USBORNE
FOOTBALL SKILLS

Katie Daynes and Simon Tudhope

Photography by
Alexandra Johnson
Illustrated by Fran Bueno
Designed by Krysia Ellis

With expert advice from
professional footballer
Naomi Bedeau

In association with
Show Racism the Red Card

CONTENTS

4 Intro

Ball control

6 First touch
8 Foot control
10 Keepy uppies
12 Chest control
14 Dribbling
16 Shielding the ball
18 Feinting
20 Trick turns
22 Heel tricks
24 Freestyle tricks

Passing & shooting

26 Push pass
28 One-two
30 Crossing
32 Low instep drive
34 Lofted pass
36 Inside foot swerve
38 Outside foot swerve
40 Front volley
42 Side volley
44 Chipping
46 Placing a shot
48 Striking the ball
50 Beating the keeper

Defending

52 Jockeying
54 Intercepting
56 Block tackle
58 Slide tackle
60 Forming a wall
62 Team communication

Set plays

64 Throw-in technique
66 Long throw-ins
68 Corner kick
70 Driven corner
72 Bending a free kick
74 Free kick tricks
76 Penalties

Goalkeeping

78 Goalkeeper's stance
80 Shot stopping
82 Collapsing save
84 Diving save
86 Narrowing the angle
88 One-on-ones
90 Dealing with crosses
92 Tipping the ball

Playing together

94 Being a team
96 The rules
98 Respect
100 Show Racism the Red Card

102 Glossary
104 Credits

INTRO

Football is a game that everyone can play. All you need to get started is a ball. This book describes the main skills involved and suggests drills to help you practise them.

SKILL LEVEL 8 OUT OF 10

FOR EACH SKILL THERE'S A DIFFICULTY RATING OUT OF 10.

EACH SKILL WILL MAKE YOU A BETTER PLAYER.

SOME OF THE DRILLS USE CONES OR A GOAL, BUT WATER BOTTLES AND SWEATSHIRTS CAN WORK JUST AS WELL.

USBORNE QUICKLINKS

For links to websites where you can watch video demonstrations of the skills in this book and pick up tips from professional players, go to **usborne.com/Quicklinks** and type in the book title.

QUICKLINKS Discover many websites along the way that can help you improve your skills. usborne.com/Quicklinks

Usborne Publishing is not responsible for the content or availability of external websites. Children should be supervised online. Please follow the internet safety guidelines at Usborne Quicklinks.

HOW TO HONE A SKILL

The best way to improve your game is to practise a skill again and again and again. That's what the pros do!

PRO TIP
Repeat a skill until it becomes so natural you don't need to think about it.

LOOK OUT FOR MORE PROFESSIONAL TIPS ALONG THE WAY.

TRY OUT THE DRILLS TO IMPROVE YOUR SKILLS.

IN A GAME
Read the "in a game" suggestions to learn how different skills can be used on the pitch.

WHERE TO STRIKE
There are diagrams to show you how best to strike the ball.

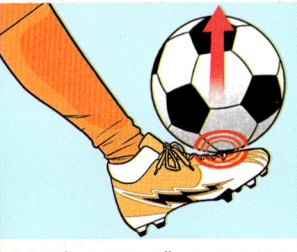

BALL CONTROL

FIRST TOUCH

Your first touch of the ball is crucial. You need to bring it under control quickly, so you're in charge of what happens next.

SKILL LEVEL 2 OUT OF 10

PRO TIP
A good first touch makes it harder for your opponent to get the ball.

MOVE YOUR FOOT TO MEET THE BALL.

KEEP YOUR LEG RELAXED, SO THE BALL DOESN'T BOUNCE OFF YOUR FOOT.

CUSHION THE BALL WITH THE INSIDE OF YOUR FOOT.

IN A GAME
If the ball bounces off you, you could lose possession. But with it at your feet you're in control.

CUSHIONING THE BALL

Cushioning the ball means taking the speed out of it, just as a cushion would if it were attached to your body.

1 POSITION THE INSIDE OF YOUR FOOT IN LINE WITH THE ONCOMING BALL.

2 RELAX YOUR LEG AND LET YOUR FOOT TRAVEL BACK WITH THE BALL.

3 THE SPEED OF THE BALL IS ABSORBED. NOW YOU HAVE IT UNDER CONTROL.

TRAINING DRILL

With a teammate, practise cushioning the ball to improve your first touch.

Position two cones a short distance apart.

Play a diagonal pass to your teammate. They cushion the ball, play it onto their other foot, then pass back to you.

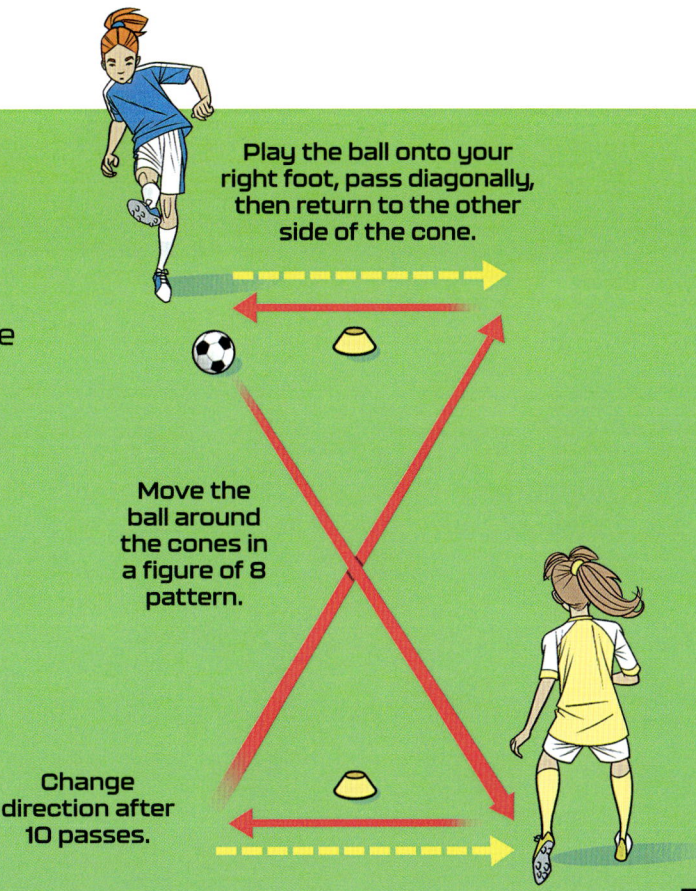

Play the ball onto your right foot, pass diagonally, then return to the other side of the cone.

Move the ball around the cones in a figure of 8 pattern.

Change direction after 10 passes.

BALL CONTROL

FOOT CONTROL

Often the ball will reach you in mid-air. To control it, you can use your foot to bring it down gently.

SKILL LEVEL 5 OUT OF 10

KEEP YOUR EYES ON THE BALL AS IT DROPS TOWARDS YOUR FOOT.

GET YOUR WHOLE BODY BEHIND THE BALL.

RAISE YOUR FOOT SO THE LACES OF YOUR BOOT MAKE CONTACT WITH THE BALL.

STIFFEN YOUR STANDING LEG.

LOWER YOUR FOOT TO CUSHION THE BALL AS IT COMES DOWN.

PRO TIP
Core strength and balance drills will help you to control the ball under pressure.

HIGH BALL DRILLS

Practise controlling the ball as it drops towards you.

Start by throwing the ball straight up into the air and bringing your foot up to meet it as it falls.

Then work with a partner, taking turns to throw the ball.

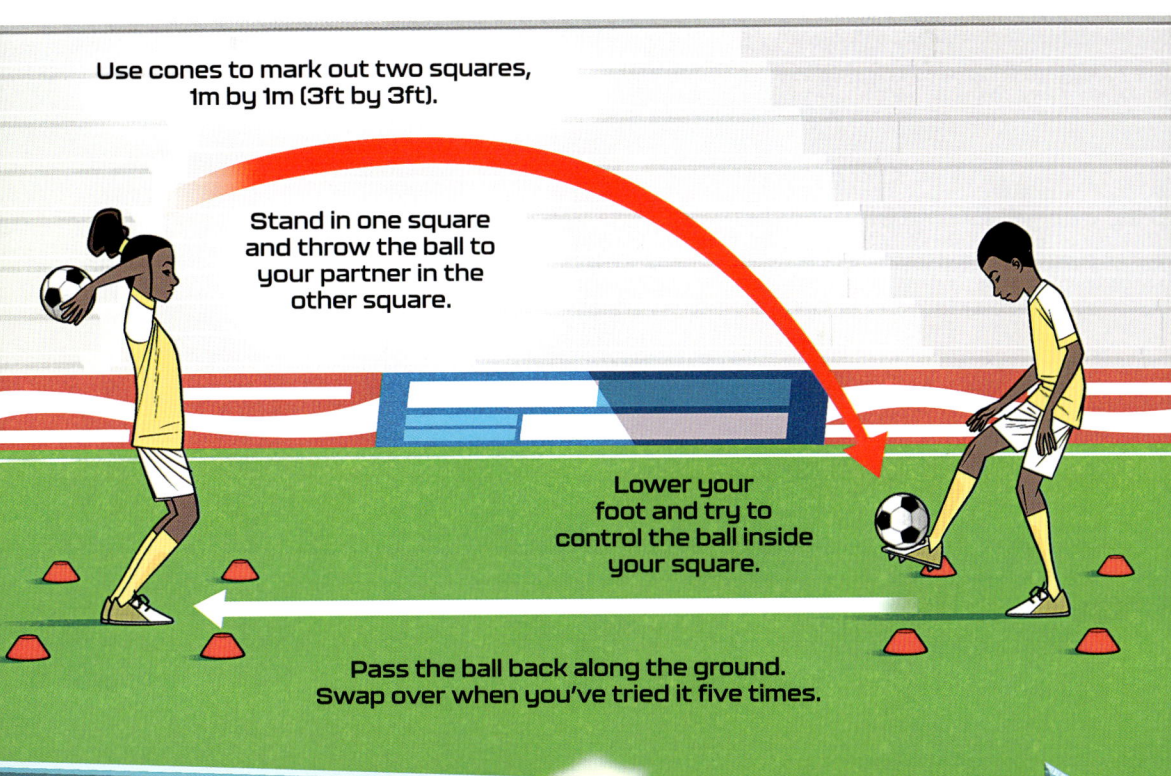

The higher the ball, the harder it will be to control.

Use cones to mark out two squares, 1m by 1m (3ft by 3ft).

Stand in one square and throw the ball to your partner in the other square.

Lower your foot and try to control the ball inside your square.

Pass the ball back along the ground. Swap over when you've tried it five times.

DRILL VARIATION

If the ball is coming straight at you above waist height, you may need to use your chest to control it instead (see page 12).

BALL CONTROL

KEEPY UPPIES

SKILL LEVEL 7 OUT OF 10

Keepy uppies, or kick-ups, are great for improving your reactions, ball control and concentration.

QUICKLINKS Find useful keepy uppy videos to help you get started. usborne.com/Quicklinks

1 DRAG THE BALL BACK AND FLICK IT UP.

Flick gently so the ball stays close.

2 KEEP KICKING THE BALL UP WITHOUT LETTING IT TOUCH THE GROUND.

Use the top of your foot to control the ball.

3 TRY BOUNCING THE BALL OFF YOUR KNEE OR SHOULDER, TOO.

Can you manage a combination of moves?

PRO TIP
You can do keepy uppies anywhere – on the beach, in the yard, at the park...

10

HOW TO GET STARTED

Don't expect to be able to do lots of keepy uppies straight away. Here are three stages that can help you build up your skills.

1 DROP WITH BOUNCE

Drop the ball, let it bounce, then kick it up and catch it. Practise with both feet.

2 DROP NO BOUNCE

Drop the ball straight onto your foot, then kick it up and catch it. Practise with both feet.

3 DRAG BACK

Place your foot on top of the ball and roll it back.

Quickly move your foot under it...

...scoop it into the air and catch it.

SET A RECORD

Once you've mastered the technique, try keeping the ball up without catching it. How many kicks can you do before it touches the ground? Keep count, then try to beat your record!

BALL CONTROL

CHEST CONTROL

SKILL LEVEL 6 OUT OF 10

Your chest is good for controlling awkward, high balls and bringing them safely to the ground.

⚠️ HANDBALL!

It's a foul (against the rules) to deliberately touch the ball with any part of your arm below the shoulder, so keep both arms out of the way.

1 PUT YOUR ARMS BACK AND OPEN UP YOUR CHEST.

Present your whole chest and lean back slightly.

2 CUSHION THE BALL BY RELAXING AS IT MAKES CONTACT.

If it's a slow ball you may need to push it forward.

3 BRING YOUR SHOULDERS IN SO THE BALL DROPS TO THE GROUND.

You want the ball to drop in front of you for your next touch.

CHEST DRILL

Do this drill in pairs to improve your chest control. Then you can use your chest in a game to set the ball up for a pass or shot.

YOUR PARTNER THROWS THE BALL SO IT LOOPS UP HIGH.

MOVE INTO POSITION TO RECEIVE THE BALL.

KEEP YOUR EYES ON THE BALL TO FOLLOW IT ONTO YOUR CHEST...

...THEN LET IT DROP TO THE GROUND AND PUSH PASS IT BACK.

SWAP OVER AFTER 10 THROWS.

DRILL PROGRESSION

Vary the angle, height and distance of the throws. Can you pass the ball back on your second touch?

PRO TIP
Keep your hands open, not clenched. It helps you stay relaxed.

13

BALL CONTROL

DRIBBLING

One of the most exciting parts of football is running with the ball (dribbling). Learn to keep the ball under close control, even when you're running fast.

SKILL LEVEL 6 OUT OF 10

PRO TIP
Keep looking up as you dribble, so you're aware of who's around you.

1 TAKE GENTLE TOUCHES WITH THE INSIDE OF YOUR FOOT.

2 USE BOTH SIDES OF YOUR FOOT TO GO FASTER.

3 TRY USING BOTH FEET.

KEEP YOUR HEAD AND CHEST OVER THE BALL.

SPEED UP AND SLOW DOWN TO PUT YOUR OPPONENTS OFF-BALANCE.

KEEP THE BALL CLOSE.

DRIBBLING DRILL

To dribble past your opponents, you'll often need to change direction. You can practise this by putting down cones and weaving between them.

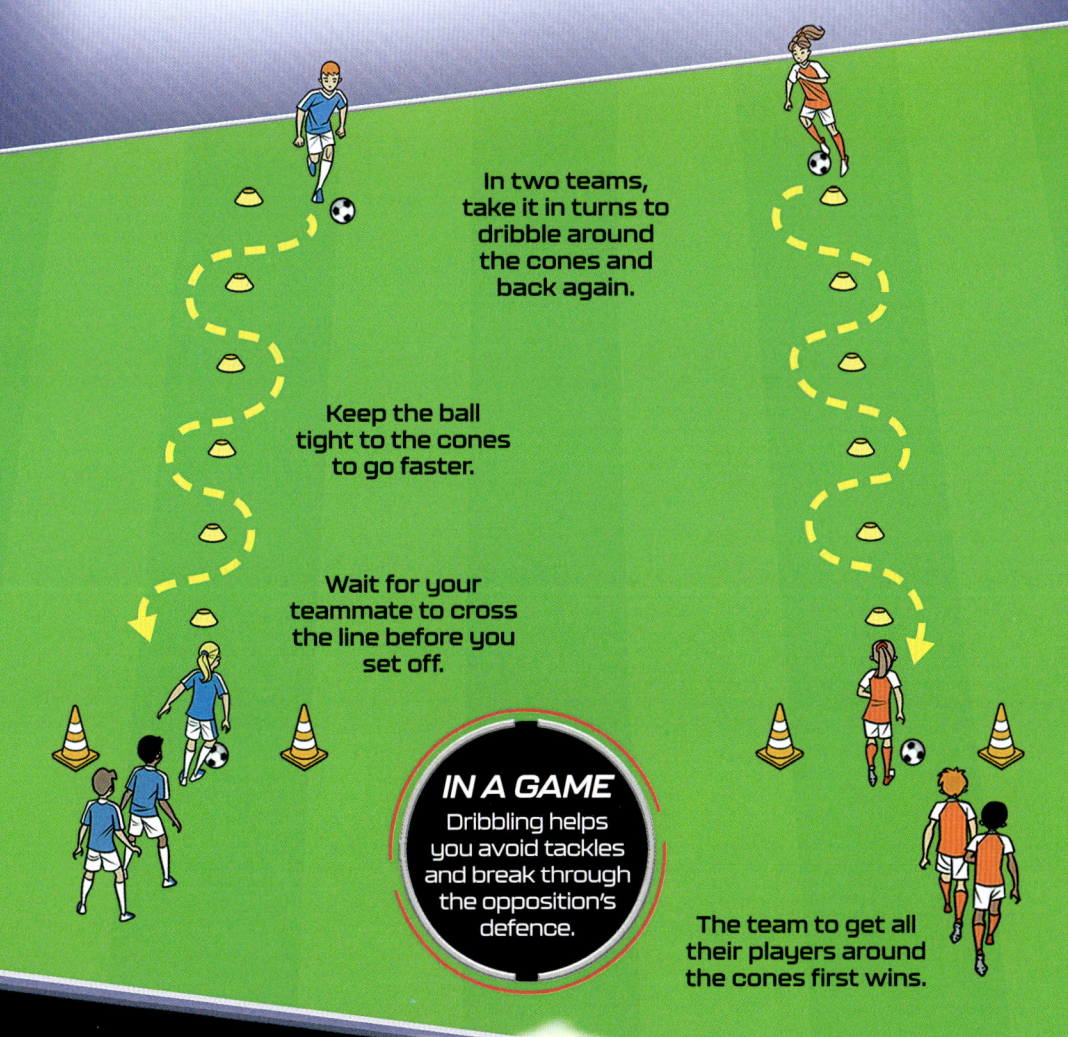

In two teams, take it in turns to dribble around the cones and back again.

Keep the ball tight to the cones to go faster.

Wait for your teammate to cross the line before you set off.

IN A GAME
Dribbling helps you avoid tackles and break through the opposition's defence.

The team to get all their players around the cones first wins.

DRILL PROGRESSION

Try the same drill, but only making touches with your right foot, then only with your left foot. You can use both the inside and outside of your foot.

BALL CONTROL

SHIELDING THE BALL

Shielding is a way of keeping possession of the ball. You use your body as a shield between the ball and your opponent.

USE YOUR ARM AND SHOULDER AS A BARRIER.

SKILL LEVEL 4 OUT OF 10

TURN YOUR BODY SO YOU'RE BETWEEN THE BALL AND THE OPPONENT.

THE OPPONENT RISKS COMMITTING A FOUL IF THEY TACKLE FROM BEHIND.

KEEP THE BALL CLOSE TO YOUR FEET.

USE YOUR STANDING FOOT TO GIVE YOU A STURDY BASE.

SHIELDING WHEN RUNNING

Watch out for opponents closing in on you, and be ready to change your body position to shield the ball.

PRO TIP

Lean into your opponent with your arm stretched out, to make a firm barrier.

IF AN OPPONENT COMES UP ON YOUR RIGHT, MOVE YOUR BODY TO THE RIGHT OF THE BALL.

IF AN OPPONENT COMES UP ON YOUR LEFT, MOVE YOUR BODY TO THE LEFT OF THE BALL.

IN A GAME

If the ball comes off your opponent and is going out of play, shield it so they can't keep it in.

BALL CONTROL

FEINTING

Feinting means tricking your opponent by pretending to go one way, then going the other.

SKILL LEVEL 5 OUT OF 10

DROP YOUR SHOULDER.

THE OPPONENT WILL MOVE THAT WAY TO STOP YOU.

THEN SWERVE IN THE OPPOSITE DIRECTION AND ACCELERATE AWAY.

SELLING A DUMMY

Feinting is also known as 'selling a dummy'. You need to be confident and convincing in your movement for it to work. Practise the steps below in pairs.

1 PRETEND TO MOVE IN ONE DIRECTION WITH THE BALL SO YOUR PARTNER DOES THE SAME.

2 QUICKLY SHIFT YOUR WEIGHT AND TAKE THE BALL IN THE OTHER DIRECTION.

IN A GAME
Use feinting when you're one-on-one with the goalkeeper, to send them the wrong way.

PRO TIP
If you're the defender, watch the ball not the player, so you're not fooled.

3 SLIP PAST YOUR PARTNER, THEN SWAP ROLES.

BALL CONTROL

TRICK TURNS

SKILL LEVEL 7 OUT OF 10

If you're being closely marked, a trick turn is a great way to lose your opponent. There are several different kinds of turns. Here's how to do a drag-back turn.

QUICKLINKS
Discover more trick turns, including scissors, stepovers and drag-backs.
usborne.com/Quicklinks

1 PRETEND TO KICK THE BALL, BUT PLACE YOUR FOOT ON TOP OF IT INSTEAD.

2 DRAG THE BALL BACK BEHIND YOU.

3 SPIN ON YOUR OTHER FOOT AND LEAN TOWARDS THE BALL.

4 COMPLETE THE TURN AND ACCELERATE AWAY.

THE CRUYFF TURN

This turn was named after the great Dutch player Johan Cruyff. It's a neat way to turn 180 degrees on the spot.

PRO TIP
Keep your foot close to the ball to complete the turn in one smooth move.

1 SHAPE YOUR BODY AS IF YOU'RE ABOUT TO KICK THE BALL.

2 SWING YOUR LEG PAST THE BALL, THEN PULL IT BACK WITH THE INSIDE OF YOUR FOOT.

3 SWIVEL ROUND AND ACCELERATE AWAY.

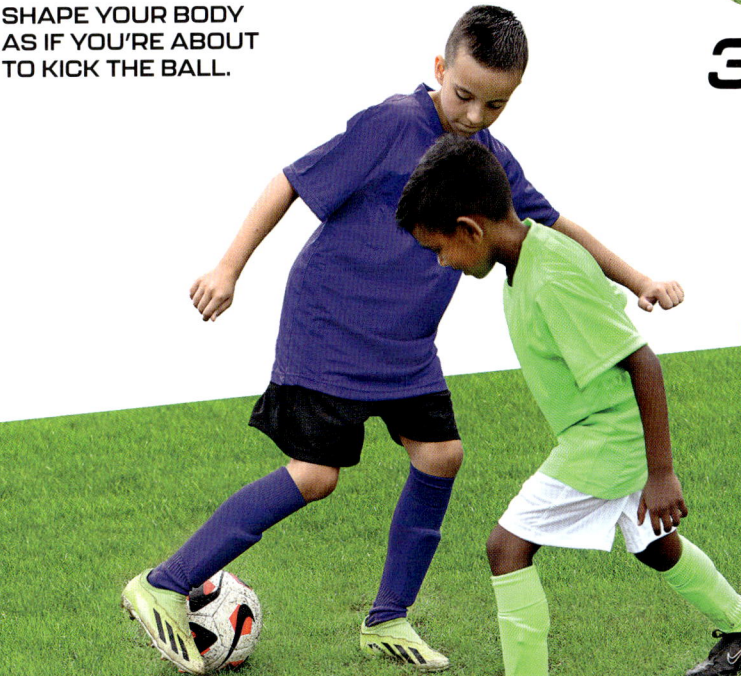

IN A GAME
A sharp turn throws your opponent off-balance and gives you more time on the ball.

BALL CONTROL

HEEL TRICKS

SKILL LEVEL 9 OUT OF 10

Heel tricks are rarely used in games, but they're fun to try and will improve your ball control, too.

THE RAINBOW FLICK

1 USE ONE FOOT TO ROLL THE BALL UP THE INSIDE OF YOUR OTHER LEG.

2 THEN FLICK IT UP AND OVER YOUR HEAD WITH THE OTHER HEEL.

3 RUN FORWARD TO MEET THE BALL AS IT LANDS.

QUICKLINKS
Watch videos of impressive heel tricks in action, including the rainbow flick.
usborne.com/Quicklinks

THE HEEL CATCH

1 WHILE THE BALL IS IN THE AIR, MOVE IN FRONT OF IT AND LEAN FORWARD.

2 BEND YOUR LEG AND CATCH THE BALL BETWEEN YOUR HEEL AND YOUR BOTTOM.

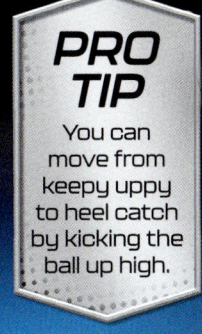

PRO TIP
You can move from keepy uppy to heel catch by kicking the ball up high.

3 TO RELEASE THE BALL, SWING YOUR LEG FORWARD.

4 CAN YOU KEEP THE BALL IN THE AIR BY ADDING SOME KEEPY UPPIES?

Heel tricks are great freestyle moves. Turn the page to find out more about freestyle football, and learn some extra tricks.

BALL CONTROL

FREESTYLE TRICKS

Freestyle football is the art of juggling a football using fancy flicks and tricks to show off your control.

SKILL LEVEL 9 OUT OF 10

'AROUND THE WORLD' IS A GOOD TRICK TO PRACTISE.

FLICK THE BALL UP AND MOVE YOUR FOOT AROUND IT IN A COMPLETE CIRCLE.

THEN FLICK THE BALL UP AGAIN WITH THE SAME FOOT BEFORE IT TOUCHES THE GROUND.

QUICKLINKS Watch freestyle footballers perform an amazing range of skills and tricks. usborne.com/Quicklinks

FIND YOUR OWN STYLE

There's no limit to the tricks and combinations you can try. Freestyle football is a sport in itself, with competitions all over the world.

PRO TIP
Try performing a range of tricks to music, and really get into a flow.

EXPERIMENT WITH DIFFERENT MOVES. IT'S GREAT FOR IMPROVING BALANCE AND CONTROL.

SITTING TRICKS ARE KNOWN AS SIT-DOWNS. PUT YOUR HANDS ON THE GROUND FOR SUPPORT.

PASSING & SHOOTING

PUSH PASS

SKILL LEVEL 2 OUT OF 10

This is a kick along the ground to a nearby teammate. It's accurate and easy to learn.

WHERE TO STRIKE

Strike the middle of the ball with the inside of your foot.

YOUR KICKING FOOT IS ALMOST AT A RIGHT ANGLE TO YOUR OTHER FOOT.

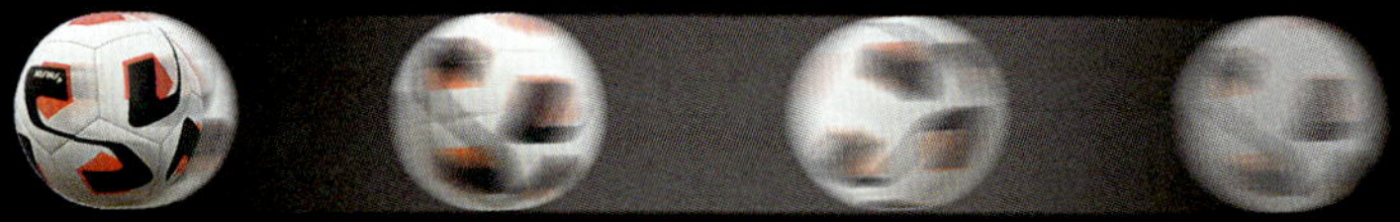

1 PLACE ONE FOOT BY THE BALL AND LIFT YOUR OTHER FOOT BACK.

2 KEEP YOUR EYE ON THE BALL AS YOU SWING YOUR FOOT FORWARD.

3 STRIKE FIRMLY WITH THE INSIDE OF YOUR FOOT.

Hold your body fairly straight.

Stiffen your ankle when you make contact.

Follow through smoothly.

PASSING DRILL

QUICKLINKS
Watch videos with passing drills plus tips on how to master the push pass.
usborne.com/Quicklinks

Work in pairs and place two markers 60cm (2ft) apart. Stand either side of the markers and pass to each other through the gap. Score a point for each successful pass.

START OFF 2M (6FT) APART.

PRACTISE BOTH RIGHT FOOT AND LEFT FOOT PASSES.

CONTROL THE BALL BEFORE PASSING BACK.

DRILL PROGRESSION

After five passes each, move another 1m (3ft) apart and start again. Carry on until you are 10m (30ft) apart. The player with the most points wins.

PRO TIP
Strike the ball firmly, so the pass is harder to intercept.

PASSING & SHOOTING

ONE-TWO

A one-two involves two quick passes between you and a teammate. It's a useful way to beat the defence and move the ball at speed.

SKILL LEVEL 6 OUT OF 10

WHEN YOUR PATH IS BLOCKED BY A DEFENDER, QUICKLY PASS TO A TEAMMATE.

YOU CAN THEN DASH PAST THE DEFENDER...

...AND RECEIVE THE RETURN PASS WITH MORE SPACE AHEAD OF YOU.

ONE-TWO DRILL

Mark out an area 24 x 6m (80 x 20ft). The player with the ball has to get past four defenders, using a mixture of one-two passes and dribbling.

PRO TIP
Call for the one-two as you pass, so your teammate knows to pass back.

The defenders make a line down the centre.

The attackers stand at the sides.

FINISH

START

Run towards each defender, and either pass or dribble around them. Keep the defender guessing!

IN A GAME
One-twos can be a great way to get the ball through a packed defence.

Swap with a teammate once you've lost the ball or reached the end.

Score a point for each defender you get past. Who can get the furthest?

29

PASSING & SHOOTING

CROSSING

A cross is a long sideways pass into the box (penalty area). If you're attacking down the wing, it's a great way to set up a goal.

SKILL LEVEL 7 OUT OF 10

SWING YOUR LEG ACROSS YOUR BODY AND THROUGH THE BALL.

HOLD YOUR ARMS OUT TO IMPROVE YOUR BALANCE.

IN A GAME
The penalty spot is a good place to aim for to give your forwards a chance to score.

WRAP YOUR FOOT AROUND THE OUTSIDE OF THE BALL SO IT CURLS IN.

A SIMILAR TECHNIQUE CAN BE USED FOR A CORNER KICK. FIND OUT MORE ON PAGE 68.

CROSS DRILL

Work on your crossing skills in a group of three. Player A passes to player B, who dribbles down the wing, then crosses the ball to player C.

PRO TIP
Cross the ball while you're still running, to give it extra power.

Rotate positions, so each player gets a go at crossing.

Use a cone to mark where the cross should be taken. You can vary its position.

DRILL PROGRESSION

Add in a player to defend the cross, so you have to curl the ball over them.

PASSING & SHOOTING

LOW INSTEP DRIVE

Your instep is the top part of your foot where your laces are. If you want to kick the ball a long way, take a run-up and use your instep.

SKILL LEVEL 7 OUT OF 10

PRO TIP
The secret to making the kick accurate is to hit the ball straight through the middle.

HOLD YOUR HEAD AND BODY OVER THE BALL.

LIFT YOUR ARMS FOR BALANCE.

SWING YOUR LEG BACK, ALMOST TO YOUR BOTTOM.

PLANT YOUR NON-KICKING FOOT NEXT TO THE BALL

PASSING DRILL

Try this drill for four players, to help develop your instep kicking technique.

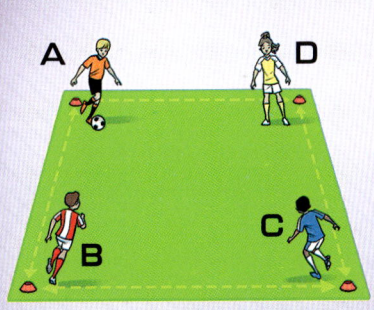

Mark out a 30m (90ft) square. The four players start in each corner.

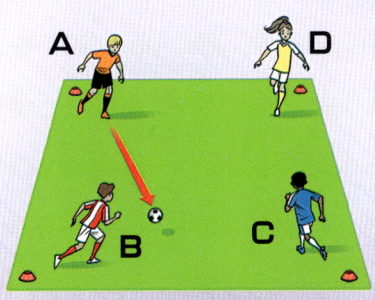

Player A passes the ball in front of B. B runs onto it and passes in front of C.

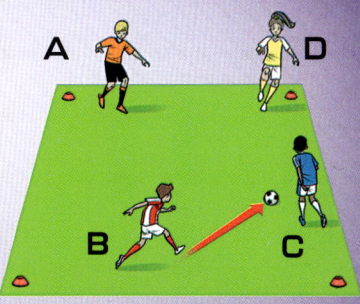

C passes to D, D to A... and the game continues around the square.

IN A GAME
The low instep drive is great for long-range passes. They're fast and direct, so hard to intercept.

DON'T LEAN BACK, AND KEEP YOUR TOES POINTED DOWN...

...SO THE BALL STAYS LOW.

WHERE TO STRIKE

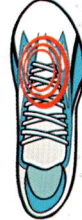

Strike the ball through the middle with your instep (where your laces are).

PASSING & SHOOTING

LOFTED PASS

SKILL LEVEL 8 OUT OF 10

The lofted pass is a long, high kick. The technique is similar to the low instep drive, but you need to get under the ball more.

1 RUN AT THE BALL, SWING YOUR LEG BACK AND LOOK DOWN.

2 MAKE CONTACT WITH THE LOWER HALF OF THE BALL.

3 SWING YOUR FOOT UP IN ONE SMOOTH MOTION.

Your instep should reach under the ball.

LEAN BACK TO GET MORE HEIGHT ON THE BALL.

WHERE TO STRIKE

Kick the lower half of the ball to make it rise.

LOFTED PASS PRACTICE

Lofted passes need to be accurate as well as powerful to reach their target. You can practise by trying to pass the ball over one or two other players.

PRO TIP
Use a lofted pass in a counterattack, to play over the defenders to your striker.

Mark out a row of four boxes, all 10m (30ft) square. One player stands in each box.

A and D try to lob the ball over B and C. They score a point for each successful pass.

IN A GAME
Lofted passes are a useful way to send the ball quickly from one side of the pitch to the other.

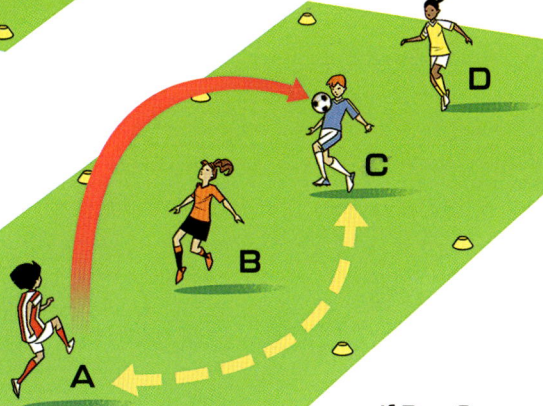

If B or C manage to intercept the ball, they take the places of A and D, and start scoring points for their own successful passes.

35

PASSING & SHOOTING

INSIDE FOOT SWERVE

Swerving or bending the ball can be really useful when passing or shooting. It's easiest to make the ball swerve using the inside of your foot.

SKILL LEVEL 7 OUT OF 10

1 PLANT YOUR NON-KICKING FOOT BESIDE THE BALL.

2 KICK THE SIDE OF THE BALL WITH THE INSIDE OF YOUR FOOT.

3 LET YOUR FOOT FOLLOW THROUGH IN LINE WITH THE CURVE.

THE BALL SHOULD KEEP FAIRLY LOW AND SWERVE INWARDS.

WHERE TO STRIKE

Kick the ball low down with the inside of your foot.

SWERVE DRILL

Practise swerving the ball by placing two cones 60cm (2ft) apart and trying to pass the ball around them. You could try this in a group of three.

Two players stand 10m (30ft) apart. The third player stands halfway between them.

The player in the middle tries to intercept the ball, but can't move outside the cones.

PRO TIP
Use the swing of your kicking leg to generate power and spin.

If the ball is intercepted or goes too wide, the player who kicked it swaps into the middle.

How many times can you pass the ball before it's intercepted?

IN A GAME
Try swerving the ball around a defender for your striker to run onto.

Practise swerving the ball one way with your left leg and the other way with your right leg.

DRILL PROGRESSION

Widen the cone area and add another player in the middle. Now you have to bend the ball even more.

PASSING & SHOOTING

OUTSIDE FOOT SWERVE

SKILL LEVEL 9 OUT OF 10

This kick makes the ball swerve the opposite way to an inside foot swerve. It's tricky to master, but very useful.

1 SWING YOUR LEG BACK AND ANGLE YOUR FOOT IN.

Hold your arm out for balance.

2 MAKE CONTACT WITH THE OUTSIDE OF YOUR FOOT.

Lock the ankle of your kicking foot.

3 USE PLENTY OF FOLLOW-THROUGH.

Sweep your leg and opposite arm across your body.

QUICKLINKS
Watch training videos with tips on how to kick inside and outside foot swerves.
usborne.com/Quicklinks

THE BALL SHOULD SWERVE AWAY FROM YOU.

38

PAIRS PRACTICE

Pass the ball to your teammate using an outside swerve. Place a marker halfway between you and try to make the ball swerve around it.

PRO TIP
Outside foot swerve is hard... which means your opponent is less likely to expect it!

Control the ball then swerve it back to your partner.

IN A GAME
This technique is great for shots and passes into the box, reaching areas the defenders think they've got covered.

WHERE TO STRIKE

Angle your foot down and strike the side of the ball with the area by your little toe.

Practise with both your right and left foot, sending the ball either side of the cone.

DRILL PROGRESSION

Try to make the ball go higher by kicking through its lower half, with your foot at less of an angle. This becomes a lofted swerve kick.

PASSING & SHOOTING

FRONT VOLLEY

SKILL LEVEL 6 OUT OF 10

A volley is when you kick the ball while it's in the air. You need quick reactions and good accuracy.

WHEN VOLLEYING AT GOAL, KEEP YOUR HEAD OVER THE BALL OR YOU'LL BALLOON IT OVER THE BAR.

1 SWING YOUR LEG BACK AND POINT YOUR TOES DOWN.

2 KICK THROUGH THE LOWER HALF OF THE BALL.

3 FOLLOW THROUGH WITH YOUR TOES STILL POINTED.

You can also volley with the side of your foot.

40

LEARNING TO VOLLEY

Work with a friend. Stand 3m (10ft) apart. Drop the ball onto your foot and volley it for them to catch.

PRO TIP
Swing your foot in a straight line or you'll slice the ball off target.

KEEP YOUR HEAD OVER YOUR KNEE.

CAN YOU VOLLEY THE BALL BACK WITHOUT YOUR PARTNER NEEDING TO MOVE?

To send the ball high, get your foot under it.

To keep the ball low, angle your foot down.

DRILL PROGRESSION

Rather than dropping the ball, get your partner to throw it to you and volley it back into their hands.

PASSING & SHOOTING

SIDE VOLLEY

SKILL LEVEL 9 OUT OF 10

To do a side volley, you need to balance on one leg while leaning sideways, then swing your leg round.

1 LEAN AWAY FROM THE BALL.

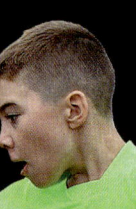

Have your arms up for balance.

2 SWING YOUR LEG ROUND TO THE SIDE.

Strike the ball with your instep.

PRO TIP

Point your non-kicking foot in the direction you want the ball to go in.

3 FOLLOW THROUGH BY SWINGING YOUR LEG ACROSS YOUR BODY.

42

VOLLEY DRILL

Find something that's almost as high as your hip, and try swinging your leg over it.

Once you've got a smooth action, try putting the ball on top and side-volleying it.

CAN YOU KICK THE BALL IN ONE CLEAN ACTION?

DRILL PROGRESSION

Practise in a group of three, taking it in turns to throw, volley or catch the ball. Score a point for each accurate volley.

IN A GAME
Keepers can throw the ball up and side-volley it for a fast, flat goal kick.

A throws the ball to B.

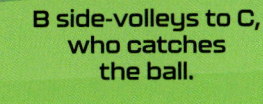

B side-volleys to C, who catches the ball.

Next, C throws the ball to A, who side-volleys it to B, and so on.

43

PASSING & SHOOTING

CHIPPING

The chip is a precise little kick that gets the ball quickly up and down. It's ideal for lifting the ball over the keeper.

SKILL LEVEL

5 OUT OF 10

1 FACE THE BALL STRAIGHT ON AND TAKE A SHORT BACKSWING.

2 BRING YOUR FOOT DOWN WITH A SHARP STABBING ACTION.

3 YOUR FOOT KICKS INTO THE GROUND AS IT HITS THE BALL.

QUICKLINKS
See some of the best chip shots made by professional players.
usborne.com/Quicklinks

THERE'S NO FOLLOW THROUGH WITH A CHIP, SINCE YOUR FOOT HITS THE GROUND.

CHIPPING DRILL

To practise chipping, you need someone to roll or kick the ball to you. See if you can chip it back over their head.

Then try this exercise in a group of three, taking turns to chip the ball over the middle player.

PRO TIP
Aim your chip so it only just clears the defender and can come down quickly.

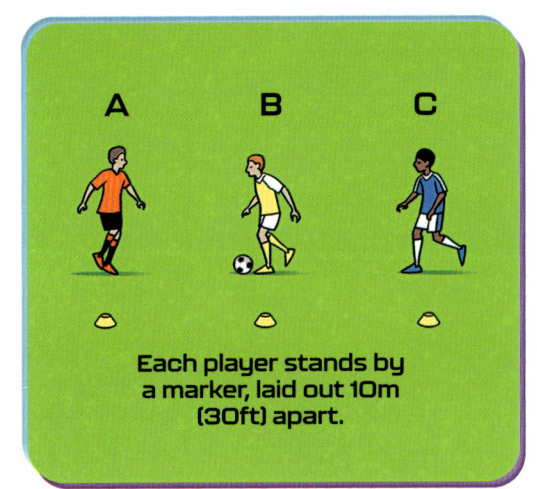

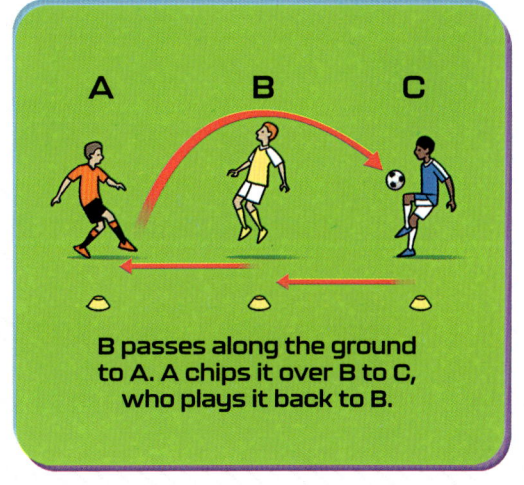

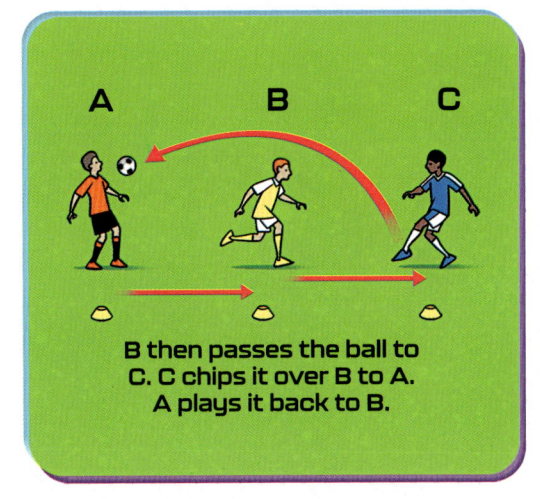

Each player stands by a marker, laid out 10m (30ft) apart.

B passes along the ground to A. A chips it over B to C, who plays it back to B.

B then passes the ball to C. C chips it over B to A. A plays it back to B.

If A or C mis-hits a chip, they move into the middle and swap with B.

45

PASSING & SHOOTING

PLACING A SHOT

To give yourself the best chance of scoring, it's important to learn how to place your shot just where you want it.

SKILL LEVEL 6 OUT OF 10

QUICKLINKS
Discover core skills to master for striking the ball with accuracy.
usborne.com/Quicklinks

PLACE YOUR SHOT WITH THE SIDE OF YOUR FOOT.

ACCURACY IS MORE IMPORTANT THAN POWER.

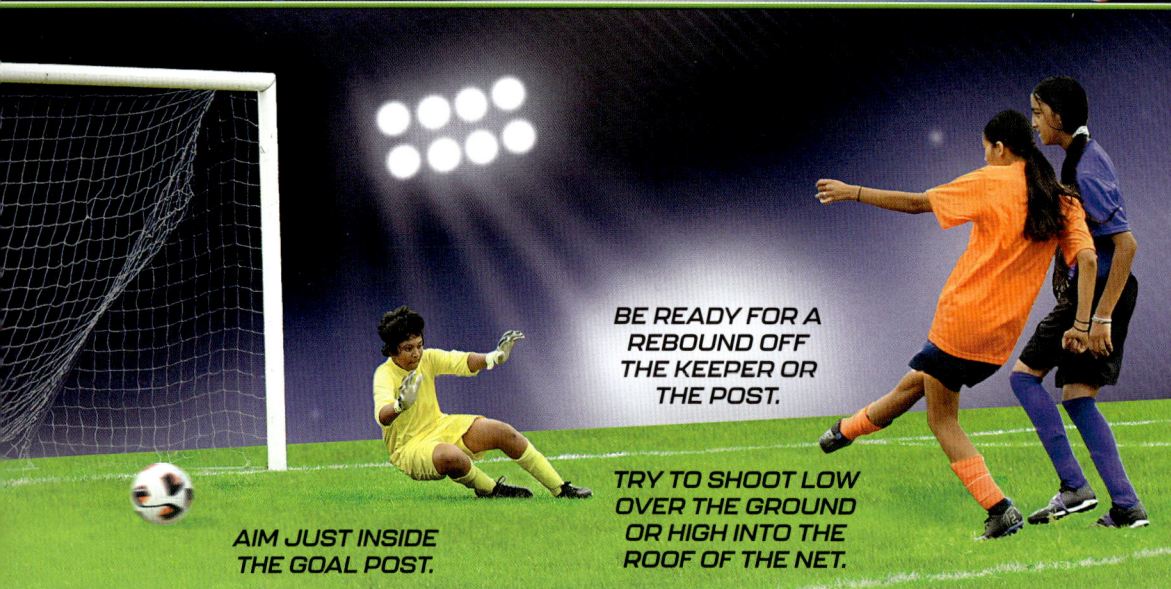

BE READY FOR A REBOUND OFF THE KEEPER OR THE POST.

AIM JUST INSIDE THE GOAL POST.

TRY TO SHOOT LOW OVER THE GROUND OR HIGH INTO THE ROOF OF THE NET.

46

TARGET PRACTICE

You can improve your aim by marking a target on a wall to shoot at, but it's even better to practise against a goalkeeper.

PRO TIP
To improve accuracy, let your leg follow through towards the target.

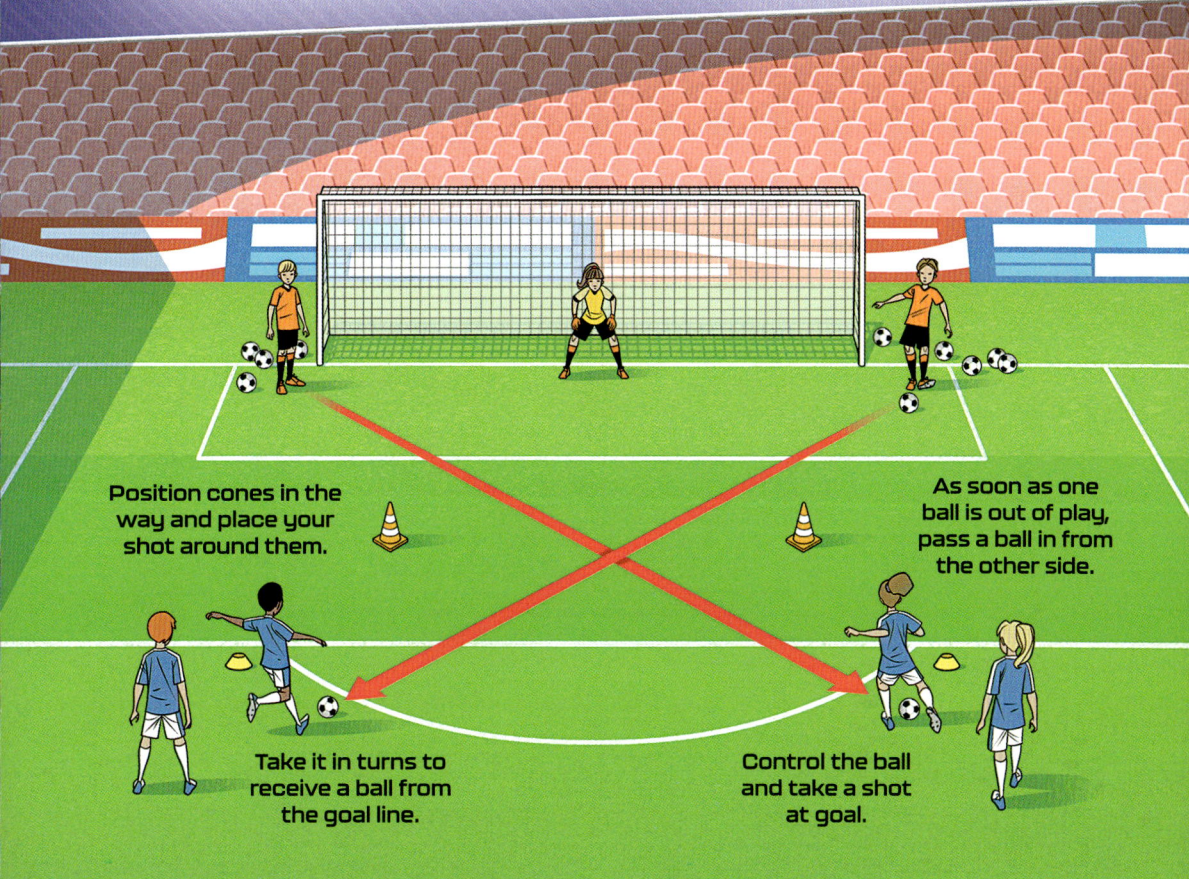

Position cones in the way and place your shot around them.

As soon as one ball is out of play, pass a ball in from the other side.

Take it in turns to receive a ball from the goal line.

Control the ball and take a shot at goal.

DRILL PROGRESSION

Replace the cones with players who will close you down as you aim to shoot. This is good practice for getting your shot off quickly.

PASSING & SHOOTING

STRIKING THE BALL

For a powerful shot, use an instep drive to strike the ball firmly and cleanly. This is also known as lacing the ball.

PRO TIP
Aim for the top corner of the goal and keep your hips facing your target.

SKILL LEVEL 7 OUT OF 10

KEEP YOUR HEAD OVER THE BALL AND YOUR EYES DOWN AS YOU KICK.

Strike through the middle of the ball to keep it under the bar.

POINT YOUR TOES DOWN, SO YOU MAKE CONTACT WITH YOUR INSTEP.

PLANT YOUR NON-KICKING FOOT NEXT TO THE BALL.

STRIKE DRILLS

First, practise your technique on a stationary ball. You could aim at a rebound fence, so the ball doesn't go too far.

QUICKLINKS
Find more strike drills that you can try out to improve your accuracy.
usborne.com/Quicklinks

Place your ball a short distance from the fence. Take a short run up... and strike it hard.

You could pick a point on the fence to aim for.

Alternatively, aim at a wall and try to get the ball to bounce straight back to you.

Next, try this drill with a moving ball. A player passes the ball to you in front of goal and you have three touches to score.

1 CONTROL THE BALL

2 TOUCH IT FORWARD.

3 STRIKE!

49

PASSING & SHOOTING

BEATING THE KEEPER

The goalkeeper will often rush out to block your shot. Here are some options for what to do next.

SKILL LEVEL 6 OUT OF 10

CHIPPING

Try chipping the ball over the keeper. It takes a delicate touch to get the ball up and down into the goal.

YOU'LL HAVE TO CLEAR THE KEEPER'S UPSTRETCHED ARM.

AIM CAREFULLY SO THE BALL IS ON TARGET.

BE READY TO REACT IF THE BALL REBOUNDS OFF THE KEEPER.

DRIBBLING

Try dribbling around the keeper by feinting one way then darting the other.

PRO TIP
If the keeper is outside their box they're easier to beat because they can't use their hands.

Pretend to shoot.

Send the keeper the wrong way.

Dodge past and place the ball into the empty net.

KEEP YOUR EYES ON BOTH THE BALL AND THE KEEPER'S POSITION.

THE KEEPER HAS TO TIME THEIR DIVE JUST RIGHT, OR THEY MIGHT GIVE AWAY A PENALTY.

MOVE THE BALL QUICKLY, BUT KEEP IT UNDER CONTROL.

51

DEFENDING

JOCKEYING

Jockeying means delaying your opponent's attack by getting in their way. Keep your body between them and the goal, and try to force them in a different direction.

SKILL LEVEL 5 OUT OF 10

IN A GAME
Jockeying keeps your opponent away from your goal.

KEEP YOUR EYES ON THE BALL, NOT THE PLAYER.

MAKE YOUR BODY AN OBSTACLE IN THEIR WAY.

PRO TIP
Don't rush in towards your opponent too quickly, or they'll dodge past you.

KEEP YOUR WEIGHT ON YOUR KNEES, SO YOU'RE IN A STRONG POSITION TO CHALLENGE.

GOAL

MAINTAINING PRESSURE

Practise jockeying in pairs. Try to force the other player away from goal or onto their weaker side. If they use their right foot, they're likely to be weaker on their left - and vice versa.

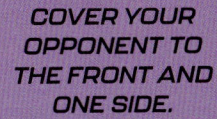

COVER YOUR OPPONENT TO THE FRONT AND ONE SIDE.

Jockeying on this attacker's right forces them to the left.

KEEP JOCKEYING TO FORCE THEM AWAY FROM GOAL.

The attacker is being forced towards the touchline.

ONCE YOU HAVE YOUR OPPONENT UNDER PRESSURE, WATCH FOR OPPORTUNITIES TO WIN THE BALL.

The defender blocks the ball out for a throw-in.

DEFENDING

INTERCEPTING

The most direct way to win the ball is by tackling your opponent, but if you can intercept the ball instead, it's easier to keep possession.

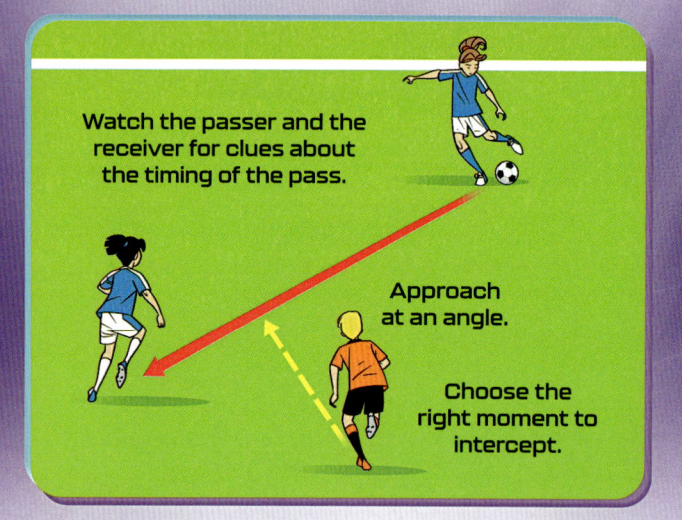

SKILL LEVEL 4 OUT OF 10

Watch the passer and the receiver for clues about the timing of the pass.

Approach at an angle.

Choose the right moment to intercept.

TIME YOUR ARRIVAL SO YOUR OPPONENT HAS ALREADY RELEASED THE BALL.

QUICKLY MOVE BETWEEN THE PASSER AND THE RECEIVER.

WHEN TO INTERCEPT

Sometimes it's better to stay between the attacker and the goal rather than trying a risky interception - because if you miss the ball, you may leave them with a clear run on goal.

PRO TIP
Look for clues to anticipate the pass. The player usually glances down just before passing.

INTERCEPTING DRILL

Try this drill for three players. One player passes to another, and the third decides whether or not to intercept.

Start by marking out a 10m (30ft) square with four cones.

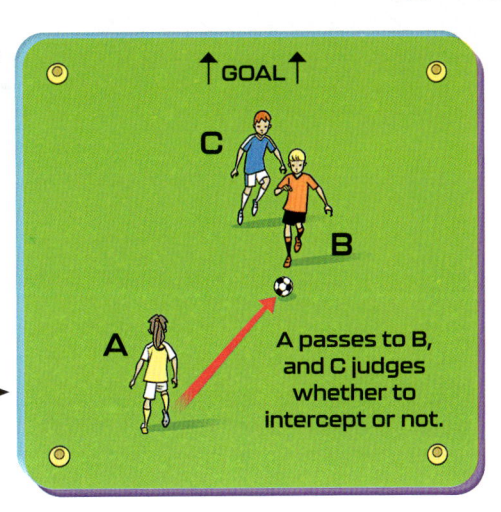

↑ GOAL ↑

A passes to B, and C judges whether to intercept or not.

OPTION 1
C decides not to intercept.

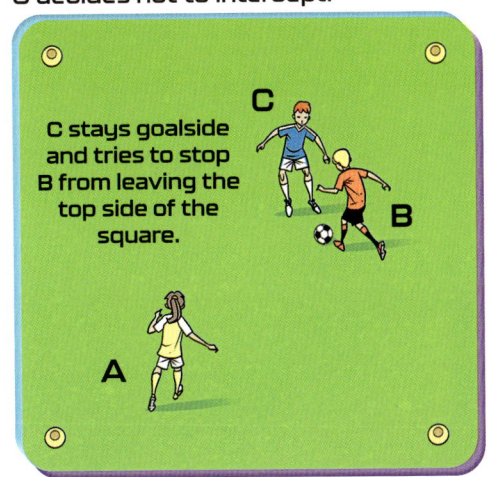

C stays goalside and tries to stop B from leaving the top side of the square.

OPTION 2
C decides to intercept.

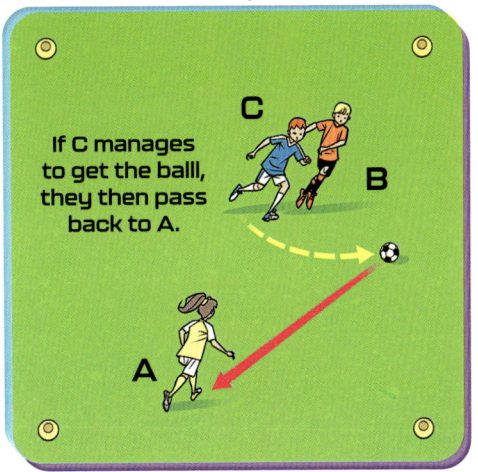

If C manages to get the balll, they then pass back to A.

55

DEFENDING

BLOCK TACKLE

SKILL LEVEL 4 OUT OF 10

To win the ball off your opponent, your tackling needs to be hard but fair. It requires good timing and a clear head. If you miss the ball or barge into the other player, you might give away a foul.

MOVE FORWARD SO YOU HAVE THE WEIGHT OF YOUR WHOLE BODY BEHIND THE TACKLE.

MAKE CONTACT WITH THE MIDDLE OF THE BALL...

...AND FORCE IT AWAY FROM THE OTHER PLAYER.

FOOT POSITION

Use the inside of your tackling foot.

TACKLE DRILL

In pairs, mark out a 10m (30ft) line. One player has the ball while the other player tries to tackle.

Start at opposite ends.

The player with the ball tries to dribble to the far end.

PRO TIP
Keep your eyes on the ball, Then you won't be tricked by any feinting moves.

The other player tries to win the ball by tackling.

Whoever succeeds scores a point.

Then the players swap roles.

TACKLING ANGLES

Use a block tackle to challenge from the front or the side.

LEAN INTO YOUR OPPONENT, BUT DON'T PUSH.

TURN YOUR WHOLE BODY TOWARDS YOUR OPPONENT SO YOUR WEIGHT IS BEHIND THE TACKLE.

IN A GAME
Block tackles are useful in a crowded situation, or when there's a loose ball and two players have an equal chance of winning it.

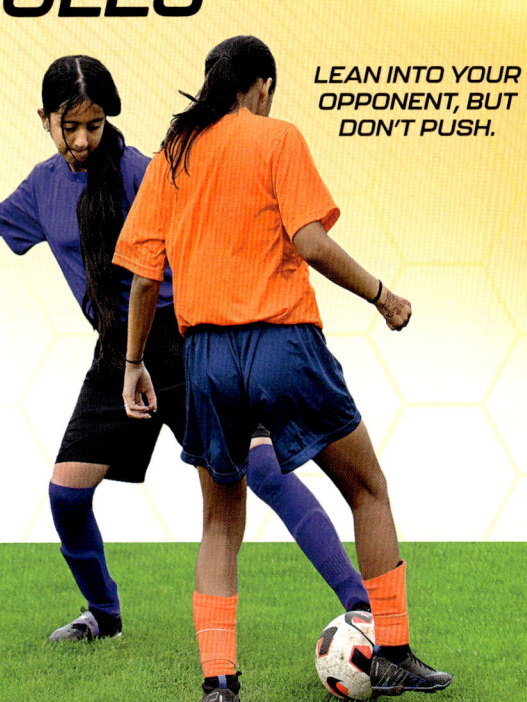

DEFENDING

SLIDE TACKLE

If you're not in the right position for a block tackle, you might need to make a slide tackle to stop a dangerous attack.

SKILL LEVEL 8 OUT OF 10

⚠️ FOUL!
It's a foul to lunge with both feet or to tackle with your studs up. The referee will award a free kick and may give you a yellow or red card (see page 96).

THE ATTACKER MAY NEED TO LEAP OVER THE DEFENDER.

SLIDE IN ON ONE LEG, WITH THE OTHER LEG STRETCHING FOR THE BALL.

NEVER USE TWO FEET TO CHALLENGE.

NEVER GO IN WITH STUDS RAISED.

KEEP IT CLEAN

Here are some tips to avoid fouling in a slide tackle.
- Be patient and wait for the right moment.
- Keep your non-tackling leg tucked underneath you, so you never slide in with both legs.
- Make contact with the ball.

PRO TIP
If you time your tackle well, you can hook the ball, spring back up and bring it away.

It's best to practise slide tackles with a cone instead of an opponent, so you're less likely to hurt someone.

PRACTISE SLIDING WITH EITHER LEG.

THE AIM IS TO SLIDE THE BALL AWAY, WITHOUT TOUCHING THE CONE.

TAKE A FAST RUN UP AND REALLY GO FOR IT.

You could practise your slide tackle timing in pairs.

Your partner passes the ball to the side of your cone.

QUICKLINKS
Watch tips on how to carry out a slide tackle safely and avoid a foul.
usborne.com/Quicklinks

You then have to time your slide to make contact with the ball but not the cone.

59

DEFENDING

FORMING A WALL

If a free kick is given in shooting range, players line up to make a defensive 'wall'. The wall covers one side of the goal, while the keeper covers the other side.

SKILL LEVEL 3 OUT OF 10

THE TALLEST PLAYER STANDS IN LINE WITH THE POST FURTHEST FROM THE KEEPER.

FORM THE WALL QUICKLY.

JUMP AS THE BALL COMES TOWARDS YOU.

STAND CLOSE, LEAVING NO GAPS.

ONE PLAYER CAN LIE DOWN TO STOP ANY LOW SHOTS UNDER THE WALL.

BE READY TO BLOCK ANY REBOUNDS.

POSITIONING THE WALL

PRO TIP
Listen to your keeper when forming the wall and follow their instructions.

For central kicks, the goal is more open so you need more defenders in the wall.

- Make sure the keeper can see the ball.
- Build a wall with four or five players.
- Don't leave an attacker unmarked.

For kicks from the side, there's less of the goal to aim at. The striker is more likely to pass the ball than take a shot.

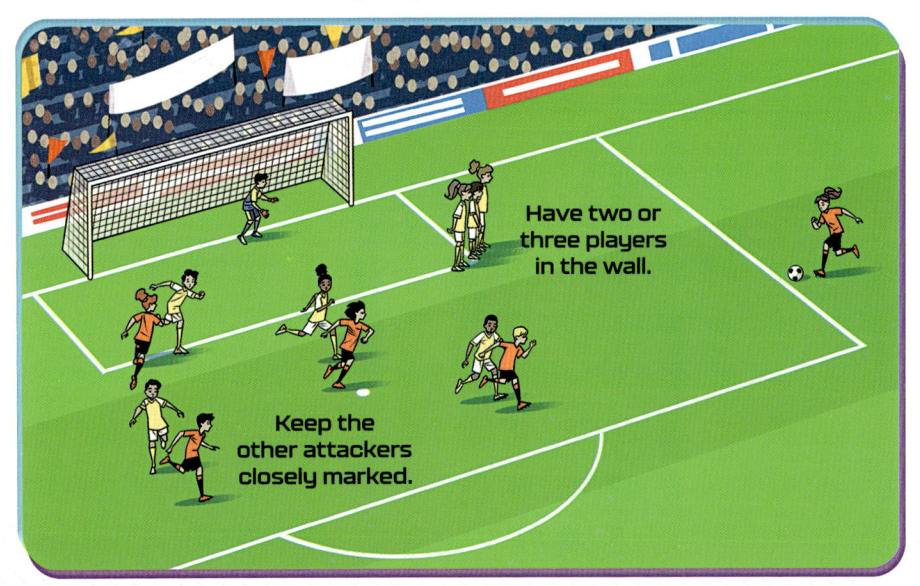

- Have two or three players in the wall.
- Keep the other attackers closely marked.

DEFENDING

TEAM COMMUNICATION

If you don't communicate well during a game, you'll end up losing the ball. Using some standard calls will help you work as a team and avoid confusion.

TANAYA'S BALL!

SKILL LEVEL 2 OUT OF 10

TANAYA'S BALL!
Shout your name to tell your teammates to leave the ball for you.

TIME!
Tells a teammate they're unmarked and can take their time.

PLAYER-ON!
Warns a teammate that an opponent is approaching.

FORCE THEM OUTSIDE!
Tells defenders to force an attacker away from the goal.

COMMUNICATION DRILL

Try this drill to practise your communication skills. Players use calls to help them attack and defend.

The players have to keep the ball within a 10m x 20m (33ft x 66ft) box.

Two defenders try to intercept the ball or make a tackle.

PRO TIP
Keep the information in your calls short and clear.

JORDAN'S BALL!

FORCE HIM OUTSIDE!

TIME!

MARK NUMBER 8!

IN A GAME
Your opponents will have numbers on their shirts, so use these to identify them.

CALL TIPS

- Only call if it will help your team.
- Use names or shirt numbers to specify who the call is about.
- Don't shout "Mine!" – call out your own name instead.
- Stay calm and don't shout over each other.

SET PLAYS

THROW-IN TECHNIQUE

When the ball goes over the touchline (the line at the side of the pitch), the team that touched it last loses possession, and the other team gets to throw it back in.

THROW THE BALL FROM BEHIND YOUR HEAD WITH BOTH HANDS.

TAKE THE THROW-IN FROM THE PLACE WHERE THE BALL WENT OUT.

SKILL LEVEL 4 OUT OF 10

THE THROWER MUSTN'T TOUCH THE BALL AGAIN UNTIL AFTER ANOTHER PLAYER HAS TOUCHED IT.

⚠️ FOUL THROW?
Follow the throw-in rules carefully, or the ref will blow for a foul throw (see page 67). And don't throw the ball straight into the goal – that's a foul too!

MAKE SURE YOUR FEET AREN'T OVER THE LINE.

KEEP BOTH FEET ON THE GROUND WHEN YOU THROW.

PRACTISING THROW-INS

Stand about 10m (33ft) apart and practise throwing the ball to your teammate's feet. Remember to release it from behind your head.

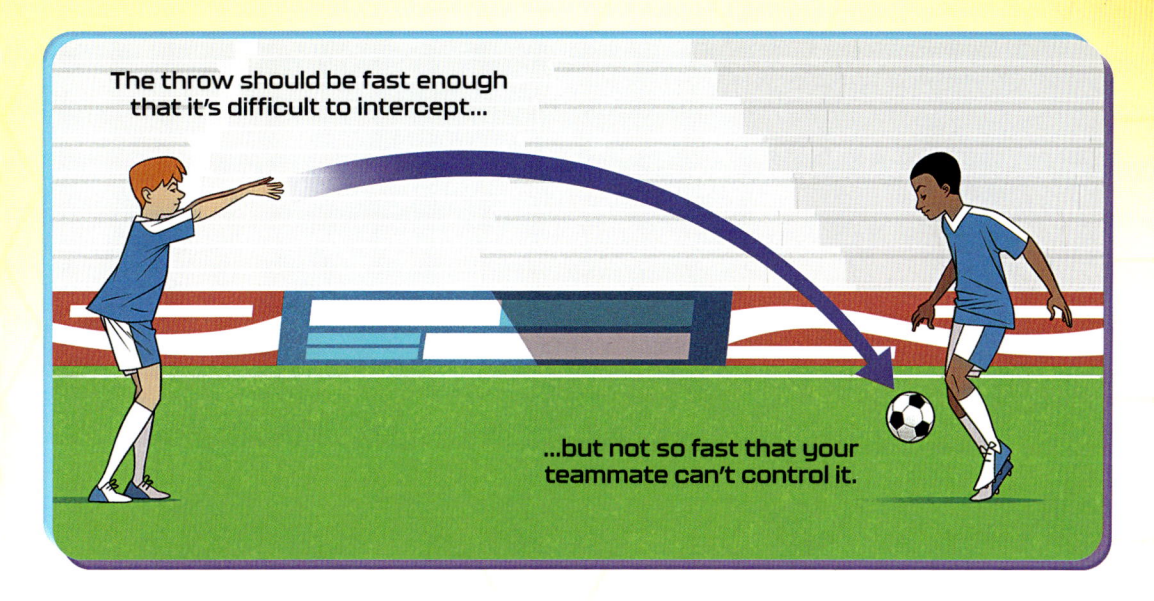

PRO TIP
You can also throw the ball into space for your teammate to run onto.

The throw should be fast enough that it's difficult to intercept...

...but not so fast that your teammate can't control it.

As you get better at throwing the ball, try aiming at different targets to improve your accuracy.

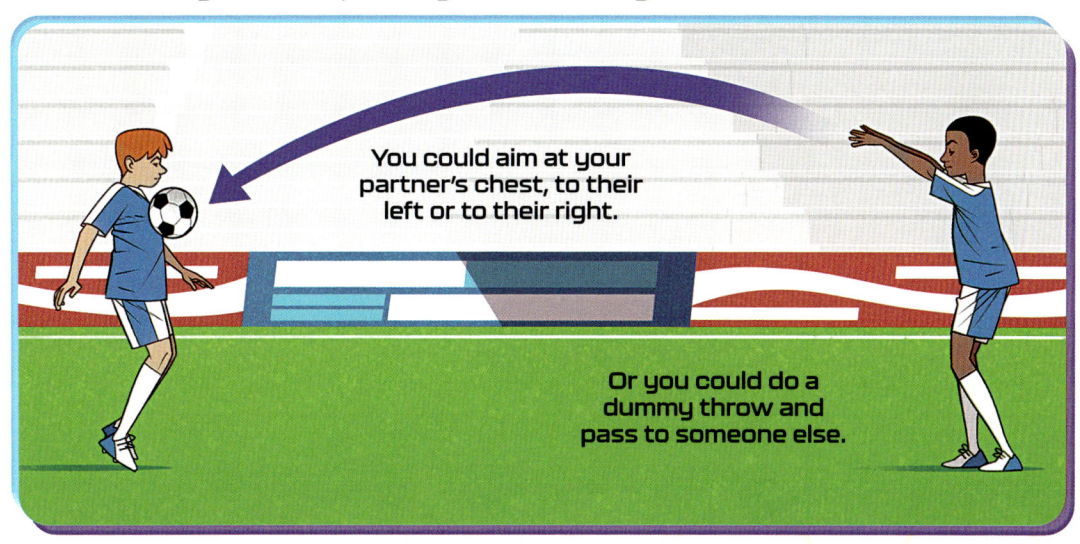

You could aim at your partner's chest, to their left or to their right.

Or you could do a dummy throw and pass to someone else.

65

SET PLAYS

LONG THROW-INS

Some teams have a player who specialises in throwing the ball a long way. You can practise this technique to develop a long, accurate throw-in.

SKILL LEVEL 6 OUT OF 10

1 TAKE A COUPLE OF QUICK STEPS FORWARD.

Judge your runup to stop before the line.

2 PLANT YOUR FRONT FOOT JUST BEHIND THE LINE AND BRING THE BALL BACK.

Arch your back to throw the ball harder.

STARTING THE THROW WITH A WIDE STANCE CAN GIVE IT MORE MOMENTUM.

3 WHIP YOUR ARMS FORWARD TO CATAPULT THE BALL AWAY.

Make sure both feet stay on the ground.

FOUL THROWS

PRO TIP
Place your hands behind the ball with your thumbs touching, to make a W.

If you break one of the rules when taking a throw-in, the referee will give the throw-in to the other team. The pictures below show how you could end up throwing away possession.

FOUL THROW!
Your feet are fully over the line. They must be on or behind the line.

FOUL THROW!
One of your feet is off the ground as you throw. They must both be on the ground.

FOUL THROW!
The ball is too far forward. You must throw it from behind your head.

SET PLAYS

CORNER KICK

SKILL LEVEL 7 OUT OF 10

A corner is given when the ball comes off the defending team and crosses the line either side of the goal. You can pass short to a teammate, or cross long into the box.

WHERE TO STRIKE

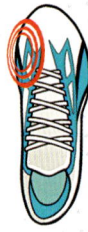

Strike the ball off-centre, so it spins as it travels through the air.

APPROACH THE BALL FROM A SLIGHT ANGLE.

LEAN BACK AS YOU KICK...

...AND FOLLOW THROUGH.

PLACE THE BALL IN THE CORNER AREA.

68

BENDING LEFT OR RIGHT

PRO TIP
Aim for the edge of the six-yard box to avoid giving the keeper an easy catch.

Place the ball so that the corner flag doesn't block your run-up. If you're right-footed, using the inside of your foot makes the ball bend to the left. If you're left-footed, it will bend to the right.

Here's how a left-footed player bends the ball away from the goal.

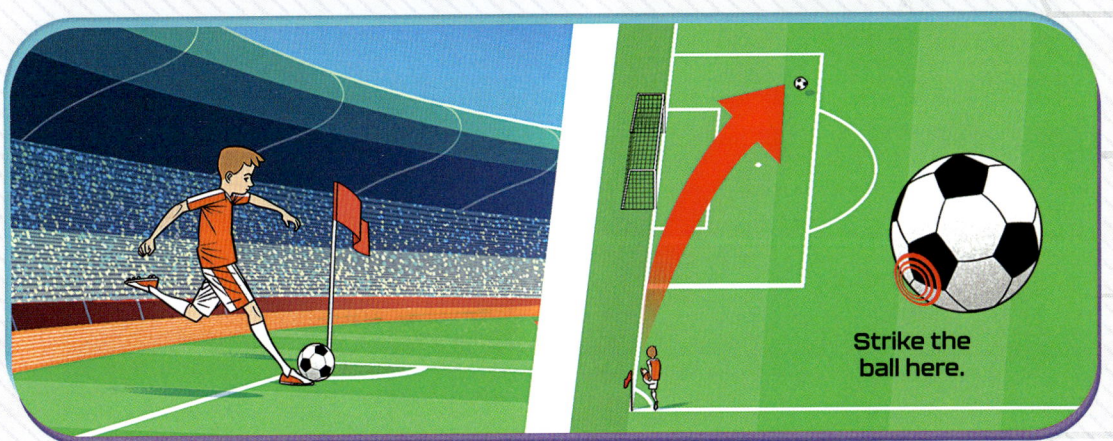

Strike the ball here.

And here's how a right-footed player bends the ball towards the goal.

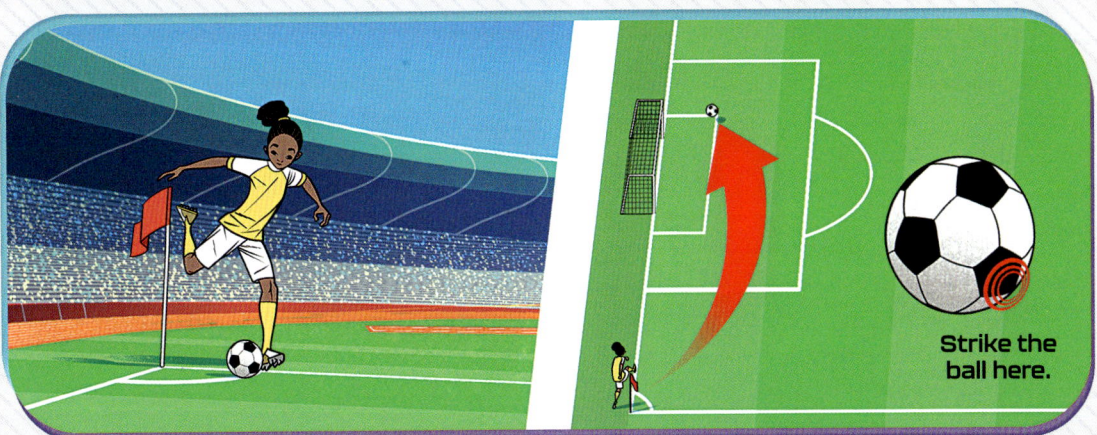

Strike the ball here.

SET PLAYS

DRIVEN CORNER

SKILL LEVEL 8 OUT OF 10

When you swing a corner in, the ball moves quite slowly because it's curving through the air. Sometimes driving the ball fast and straight can catch the other team off guard.

1 PLANT YOUR NON-KICKING FOOT AND KEEP YOUR HEAD OVER THE BALL.

2 WITH YOUR TOES POINTING DOWN, STRIKE BELOW THE CENTRE OF THE BALL WITH YOUR INSTEP.

3 FOLLOW THROUGH TO SEND THE BALL HARD AND LOW INTO THE BOX.

CORNER MOVES

Here's how a driven corner can work. Aim for a teammate on the near side of the goal.

PRO TIP
Attackers need to be on their toes, because the ball will come in fast.

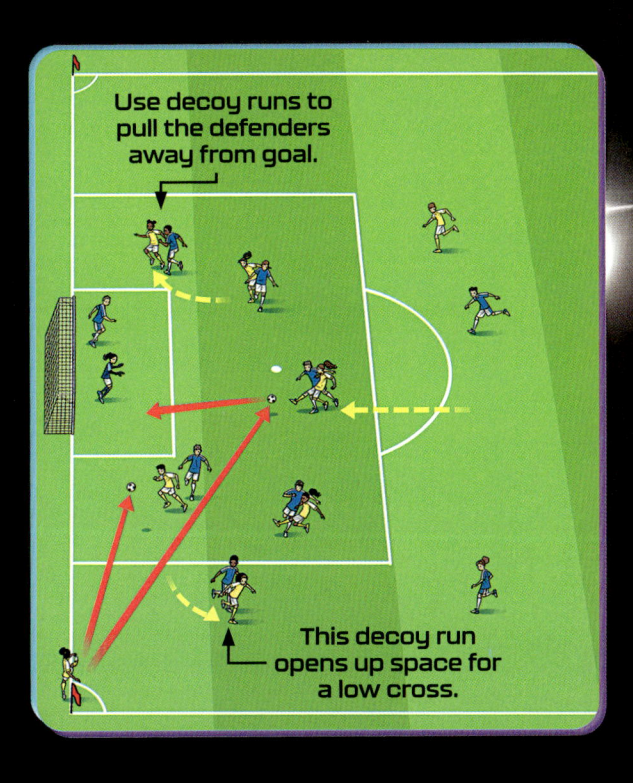

Use decoy runs to pull the defenders away from goal.

This decoy run opens up space for a low cross.

SIGNALLING THE MOVE

Signal what kind of cross you're about to do, so your teammates know where to move. Decide on the signals together in training, so the other team don't know what they mean.

71

SET PLAYS

BENDING A FREE KICK

When you get a free kick near the other team's penalty area, your opponents will form a wall between the ball and the goal. To score, you need to get the ball past this wall of players.

SKILL LEVEL 8 OUT OF 10

SPREAD YOUR ARMS FOR BALANCE.

AIM FOR THE CORNER OF THE GOAL.

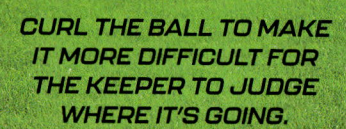

CURL THE BALL TO MAKE IT MORE DIFFICULT FOR THE KEEPER TO JUDGE WHERE IT'S GOING.

LEAN BACK SLIGHTLY TO LIFT THE BALL OVER THE WALL.

FREE KICK PRACTICE

To bend a free kick, you'll need to use the swerve techniques on pages 36 to 39. Practise bending the ball in both directions, to keep the keeper guessing.

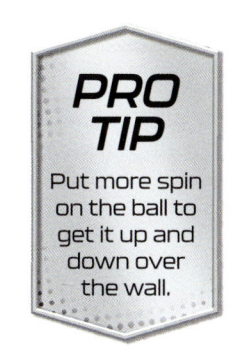

PRO TIP
Put more spin on the ball to get it up and down over the wall.

Use flag markers to help practise your swerve kicks.

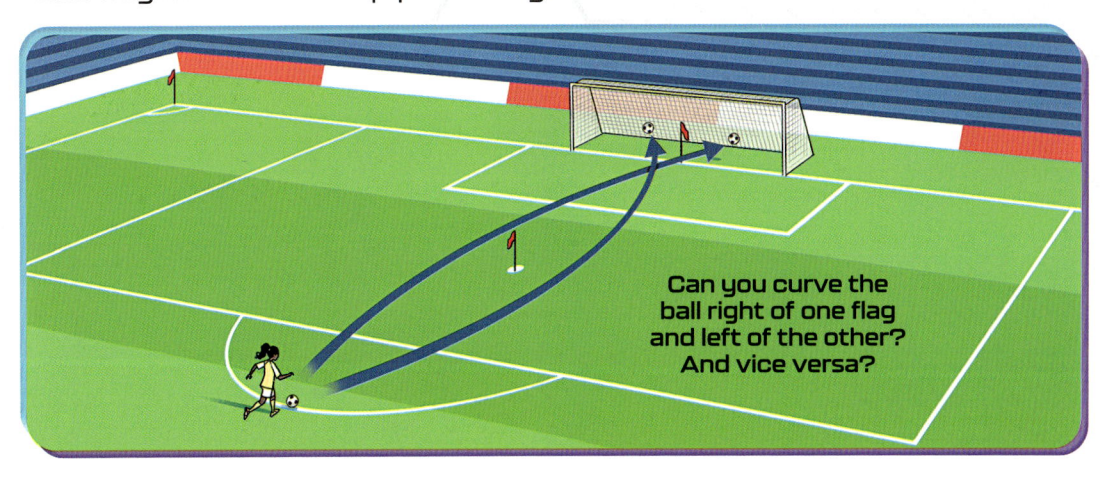

Can you curve the ball right of one flag and left of the other? And vice versa?

The inside of your foot bends it one way.

The outside of your foot bends it the other way.

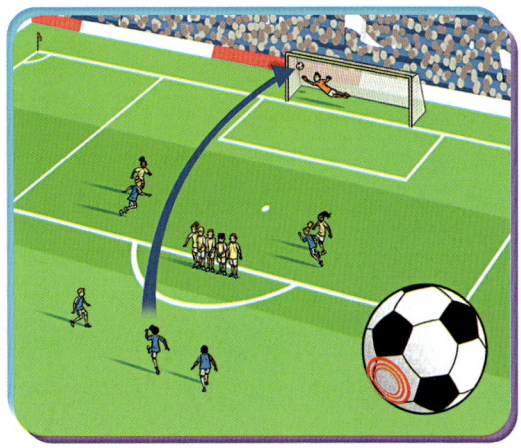

73

SET PLAYS

FREE KICK TRICKS

You don't have to shoot from a free kick. Try these tricks to surprise the other team and get past their defence.

BACK PASS SWITCH

SKILL LEVEL 6 OUT OF 10

RUN AT THE BALL AS IF YOU'RE GOING TO KICK IT...

...BUT INSTEAD, ROLL IT BACK TO YOUR TEAMMATE.

YOUR TEAMMATE CAN NOW SHOOT.

Rolling the ball back creates a better angle for the shot, because the wall and goalkeeper are now out of position.

74

DUMMY CROSS-OVERS

In this trick, one player does a 'dummy run', then leaves the ball for another player to quickly swoop in and take the shot.

PRO TIP
A dummy run can also block the keeper's view of the real shot.

1 STAND AS IF YOUR TEAMMATE IS GOING TO SHOOT, NOT YOU.

2 YOUR TEAMMATE STEPS OVER THE BALL AT THE LAST MOMENT.

3 TIME YOUR RUN TO SHOOT JUST AFTER THEIR DUMMY SHOT.

THESE DEFENDERS WILL JUMP TO BLOCK THE DUMMY SHOT.

THEY'LL BE OUT OF POSITION WHEN THIS PLAYER TAKES THE REAL SHOT.

75

SET PLAYS

PENALTIES

To score a penalty you need both skill to beat the keeper and mental strength to stay calm under pressure. Work on your aim so you can send the ball exactly where you want it to go.

SKILL LEVEL 7 OUT OF 10

1 PLACE THE BALL ON THE PENALTY SPOT, WAIT FOR THE WHISTLE, THEN RUN UP TO SHOOT.

2 FOR A FIRM, ACCURATE SHOT, STRIKE THE BALL USING THE INSIDE OF YOUR FOOT.

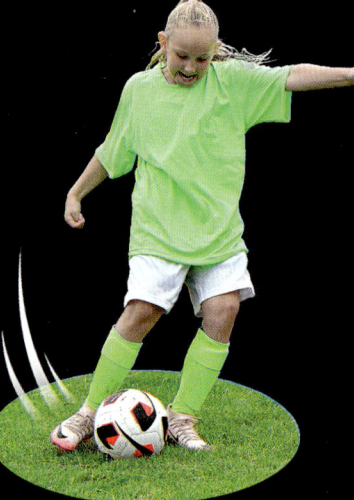

3 KEEP YOUR EYES ON THE BALL AND FOLLOW THROUGH.

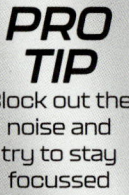

PRO TIP
Block out the noise and try to stay focussed while you wait to take your kick.

FOR A MORE POWERFUL SHOT, POINT YOUR TOES DOWN AND DRIVE THROUGH WITH YOUR INSTEP (SEE PAGE 48).

TACTICS

A powerful shot into the corner is almost impossible to save. You can also score by tricking the goalkeeper into diving the wrong way.

QUICKLINKS See how to trick the keeper and keep your cool when taking a penalty. usborne.com/Quicklinks

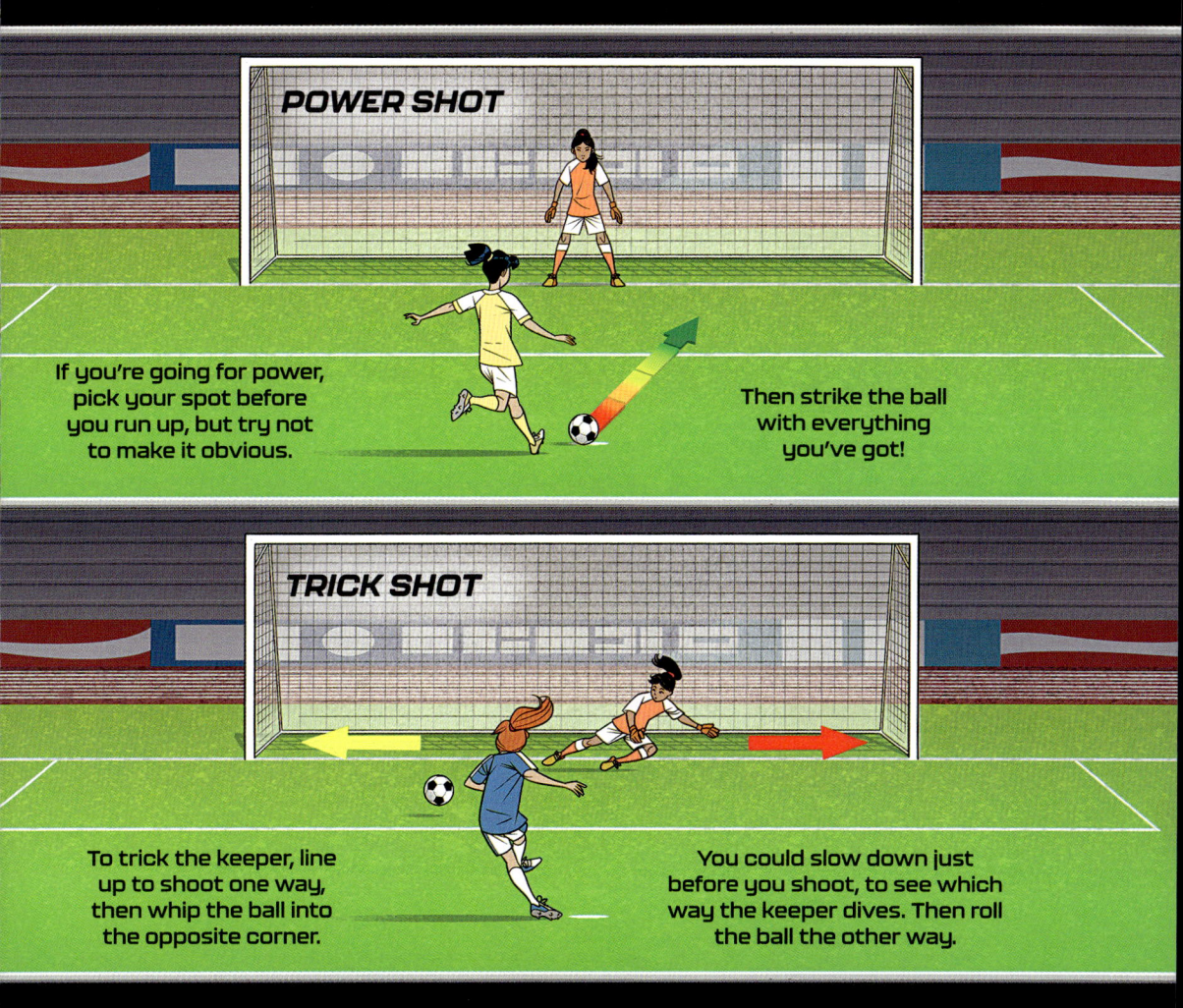

POWER SHOT

If you're going for power, pick your spot before you run up, but try not to make it obvious.

Then strike the ball with everything you've got!

TRICK SHOT

To trick the keeper, line up to shoot one way, then whip the ball into the opposite corner.

You could slow down just before you shoot, to see which way the keeper dives. Then roll the ball the other way.

KEEPER TIPS

- Try to find out about the other team's penalty taker. Do they usually shoot left or right, high or low?
- Stay on the goal line until the ball is kicked.
- Try putting the penalty taker off by staring them in the eye, or spreading your arms wide to make yourself look bigger.

GOALKEEPING

GOALKEEPER'S STANCE

If you're a keeper, you need to be alert and ready to act quickly. When the other team is nearing your goal, set yourself to spring into action.

SKILL LEVEL 2 OUT OF 10

WATCH THE ATTACKER CLOSELY FOR CLUES THEY'RE ABOUT TO SHOOT.

LEAN FORWARD SLIGHTLY AND BEND YOUR KNEES.

HAVE YOUR HANDS READY, AT ROUGHLY WAIST HEIGHT.

KEEP YOUR WEIGHT BALANCED SO YOU CAN DIVE TO EITHER SIDE.

SHIFT YOUR WEIGHT TO THE BALLS OF YOUR FEET.

CATCHING THE BALL

PRO TIP
Keep your arms relaxed so the ball doesn't bounce out of your hands.

For high balls into the box, the best catching technique is the W shape.

The palms of your hands face outwards and your index fingers and thumbs form a 'W' around the back of the ball.

EYES ON THE BALL

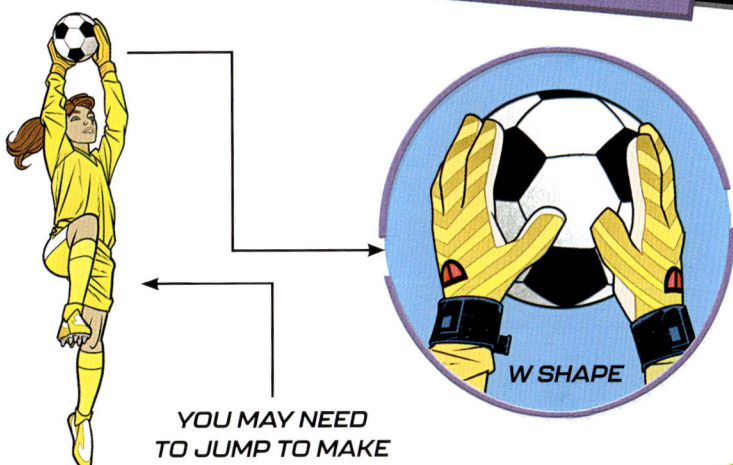

W SHAPE

YOU MAY NEED TO JUMP TO MAKE THE CATCH.
(See page 90 for more on high catches.)

CATCHING PRACTICE

Practise catching shots while keeping on the move.

Lay out a zigzag pattern of markers, 2m (6ft) apart.

Weave through the markers, staying in your stance.

A teammate chips the ball towards you.

Throw the ball back so they can take another shot.

79

GOALKEEPING

SHOT STOPPING

The best position for stopping a shot depends on how high and fast it is. Here are some options.

SCOOPING

Scooping, or cradling, is the safest way to catch a ball at waist or stomach height.

SKILL LEVEL 5 OUT OF 10

LEAN INTO THE SHOT SO YOU'RE NOT KNOCKED OFF BALANCE.

JUMP TO GET YOUR CHEST BEHIND HIGHER SHOTS.

1 ANGLE YOUR ARMS DOWNWARDS TO LET THE BALL ROLL INTO YOUR CHEST.

2 WRAP YOUR HANDS AROUND THE BALL, CLUTCHING IT TO YOUR CHEST.

THE BENDING SCOOP

For balls along the ground, bend down and scoop them into your hands.

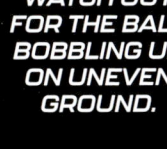

WATCH OUT FOR THE BALL BOBBLING UP ON UNEVEN GROUND.

KEEP YOUR FEET TOGETHER, IN CASE THE BALL SLIPS THROUGH YOUR HANDS.

BARRIER POSITION

If you have time to get your knee to the ground, you can create an extra barrier with your leg.

WATCH THE BALL ALL THE WAY INTO YOUR HANDS.

ONLY COMMIT TO THIS POSITION IF YOU HAVE A CLEAR VIEW OF THE BALL.

PRO TIP
Cup your hands around the ball and quickly lift it away from attackers.

GOALKEEPING

COLLAPSING SAVE

If you don't have time to move in line with the ball and scoop it up, it's best to 'collapse' behind it.

SKILL LEVEL 6 OUT OF 10

1 STEP TO THE SIDE AND LET YOUR KNEES COLLAPSE UNDER YOU.

2 GET YOUR BODY BEHIND THE BALL AND WRAP YOUR HANDS AROUND IT.

3 BRING YOUR KNEES UP TO PROTECT YOURSELF IN A CROWDED GOAL AREA.

KEEP YOUR HANDS AND ARMS FREE TO GRAB THE BALL.

COLLAPSING PRACTICE

Mark out a smaller goal size for your teammate to aim at and try to save their shots with your hands.

PRO TIP
Practise collapsing saves often. They're harder than they sound!

Do you find it harder diving to one side than the other? If so, ask your teammate to target that side.

Having several balls is useful, for taking quick-fire shots.

COLLAPSING SAVE TIPS

- Get down to the ground as quickly as possible.
- Avoid doing acrobatic leaps that might let the ball through.
- Use your hands to stop the ball squeezing under you.

GOALKEEPING

DIVING SAVE

You'll often have to dive to reach a well struck shot. Keep your eyes on the ball all the way.

SKILL LEVEL 8 OUT OF 10

1 TRANSFER YOUR WEIGHT IN THE DIRECTION OF THE SHOT.

2 SPRING SIDEWAYS INTO THE PATH OF THE BALL.

3 GRASP THE BALL TIGHTLY OR PUSH IT AWAY TO THE SIDE.

DIVING SAVE DRILLS

Here are two ways to practise diving – falling to one side and twisting around.

PRO TIP
Reach out with both hands, then extend one to cover more distance.

FALLING TO ONE SIDE

One player rolls the ball a metre (3 ft) either side of the other player.

Crouch down, then fall on your side as you catch the ball.

TWISTING AROUND

In pairs, one player rolls the ball through the other's legs.

Quickly turn and fall on the ball before it's out of reach.

GOALKEEPING

NARROWING THE ANGLE

If you stay back, an attacker has more of the goal to aim at.

Here, the attacker has a clear view of goal.

SKILL LEVEL

6 OUT OF 10

By moving forward, you narrow the attacker's shooting angles, and make it easier to save their shot.

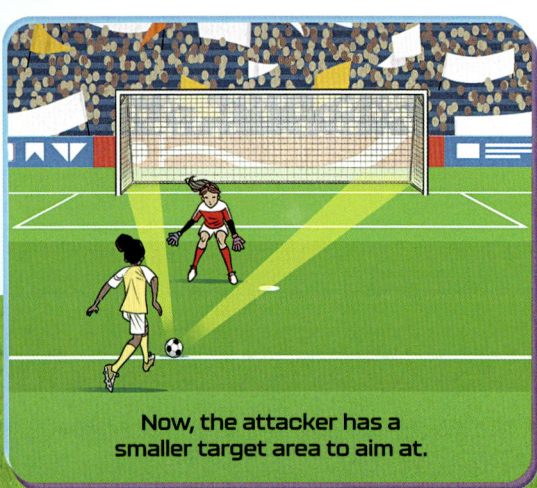

Now, the attacker has a smaller target area to aim at.

KEEP ON YOUR TOES, READY TO SPRING INTO ACTION.

86

ALTERNATING ANGLES

Practise coming forward to narrow the angles by asking two teammates to stand on either side of the penalty area.

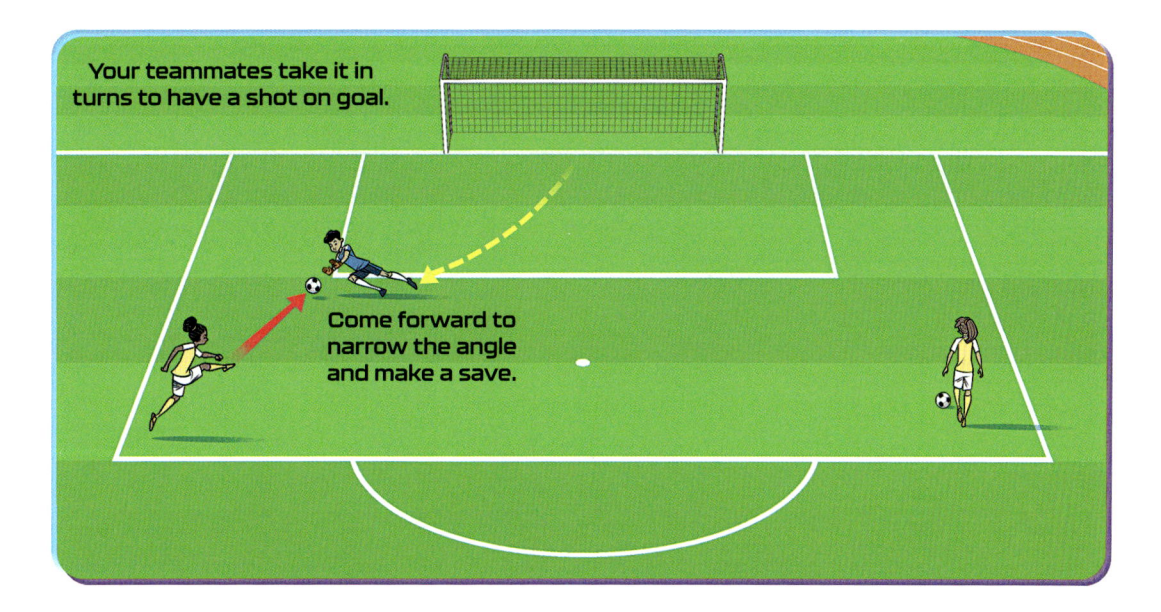

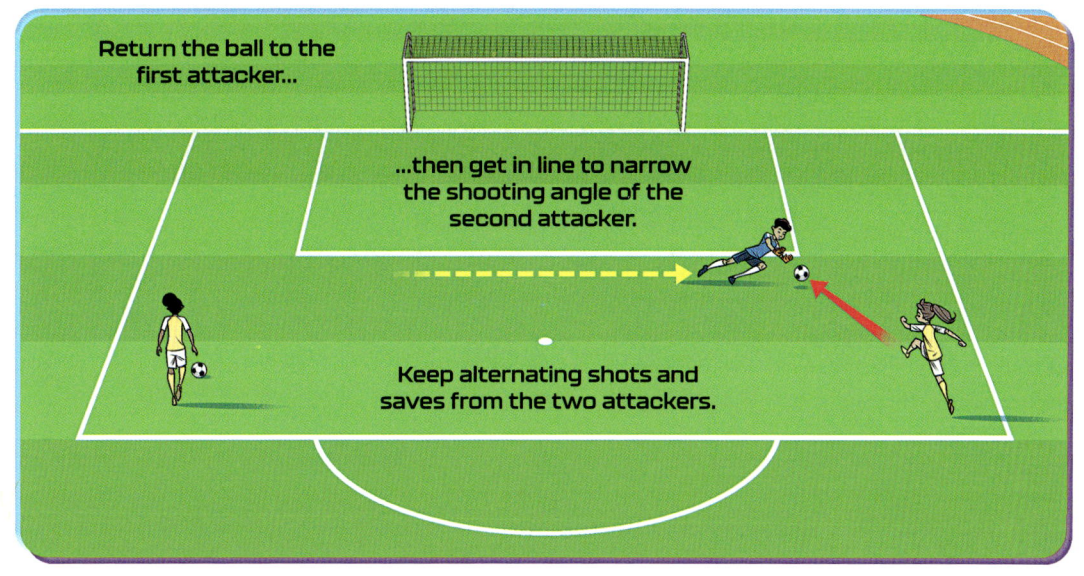

PRO TIP
Always know where your goal is! You can use the penalty spot as a marker.

Your teammates take it in turns to have a shot on goal.

Come forward to narrow the angle and make a save.

Return the ball to the first attacker...

...then get in line to narrow the shooting angle of the second attacker.

Keep alternating shots and saves from the two attackers.

GOALKEEPING

ONE-ON-ONES

SKILL LEVEL 7 OUT OF 10

When there are no defenders to help you out, rush forward to block the attacker's route to goal.

1 WATCH FOR THE BALL COMING THROUGH AND RUN FORWARD.

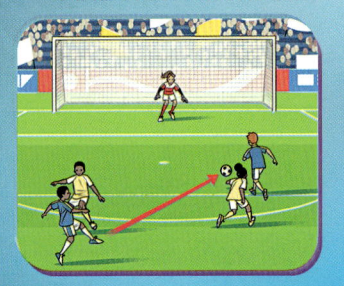

2 SLOW DOWN ONCE THE ATTACKER HAS THE BALL.

3 STAY ON YOUR FEET AND TRY TO FORCE THEM WIDE.

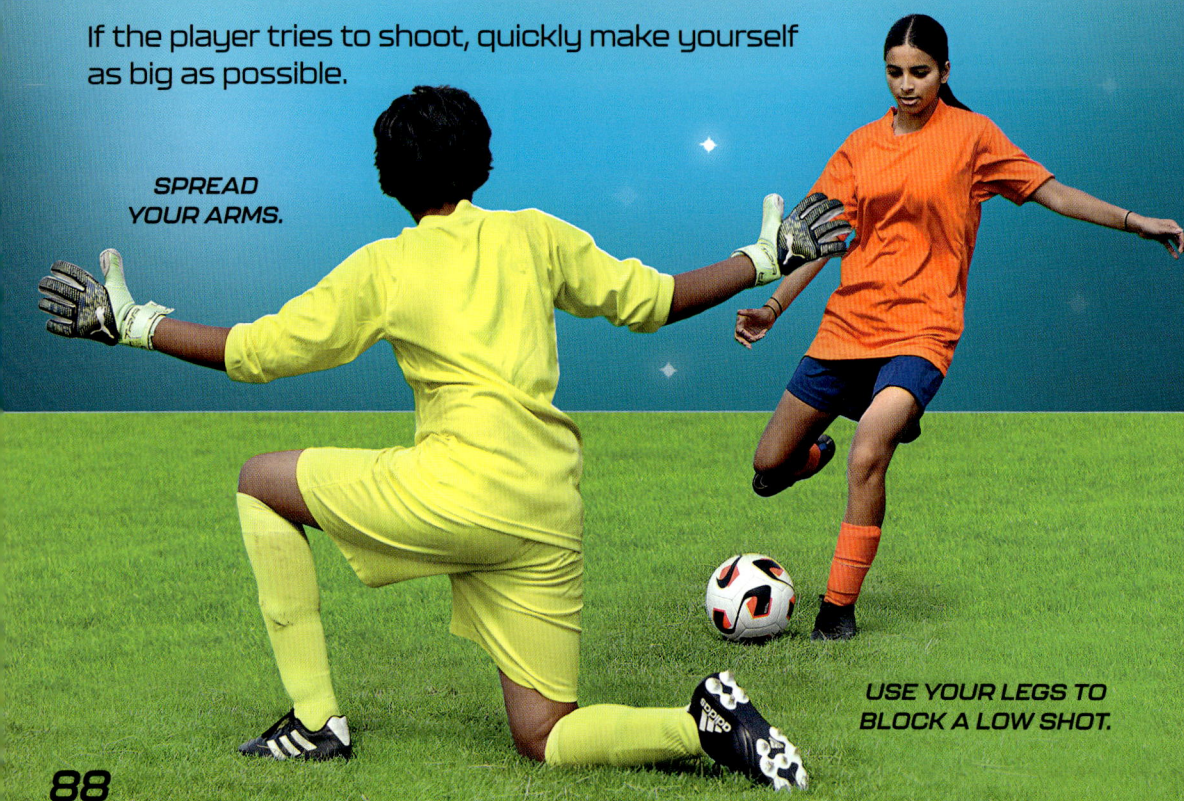

If the player tries to shoot, quickly make yourself as big as possible.

SPREAD YOUR ARMS.

USE YOUR LEGS TO BLOCK A LOW SHOT.

DIVING AT THEIR FEET

When an attacker attempts to dribble around you, one option is to dive at their feet. Only do this if you feel confident you'll win the ball.

PRO TIP
Be bold. The sight of an on-rushing keeper can put the attacker off their stride.

TRY TO GRAB THE BALL OR PUSH IT AWAY FROM THE ATTACKER.

KEEP YOUR FACE AWAY FROM THE PLAYER'S FEET.

FOUL!
Be sure to make contact with the ball first. If you catch the player first, it's a foul. If the foul happens inside the box, the referee will award a penalty kick.

WRAP YOUR BODY AROUND THE BALL FOR EXTRA PROTECTION.

GOALKEEPING

DEALING WITH CROSSES

Be ready to defend high crosses by catching the ball or punching it away.

SKILL LEVEL 7 OUT OF 10

BEAT OPPONENTS TO THE BALL BY CATCHING IT ABOVE THEIR HEADS. (THEY CAN'T USE THEIR HANDS!)

QUICKLINKS
Catch or punch? Discover how to handle crosses like a pro.
usborne.com/Quicklinks

KEEPER'S BALL!

SHOUT FOR THE BALL SO YOUR DEFENDERS KNOW TO LEAVE IT TO YOU.

LIFT THE LEG NEAREST TO THE ATTACKERS TO PROTECT YOUR BODY AGAINST CHALLENGES.

JUMP OFF ONE LEG TO CATCH THE BALL.

PUNCHING CROSSES

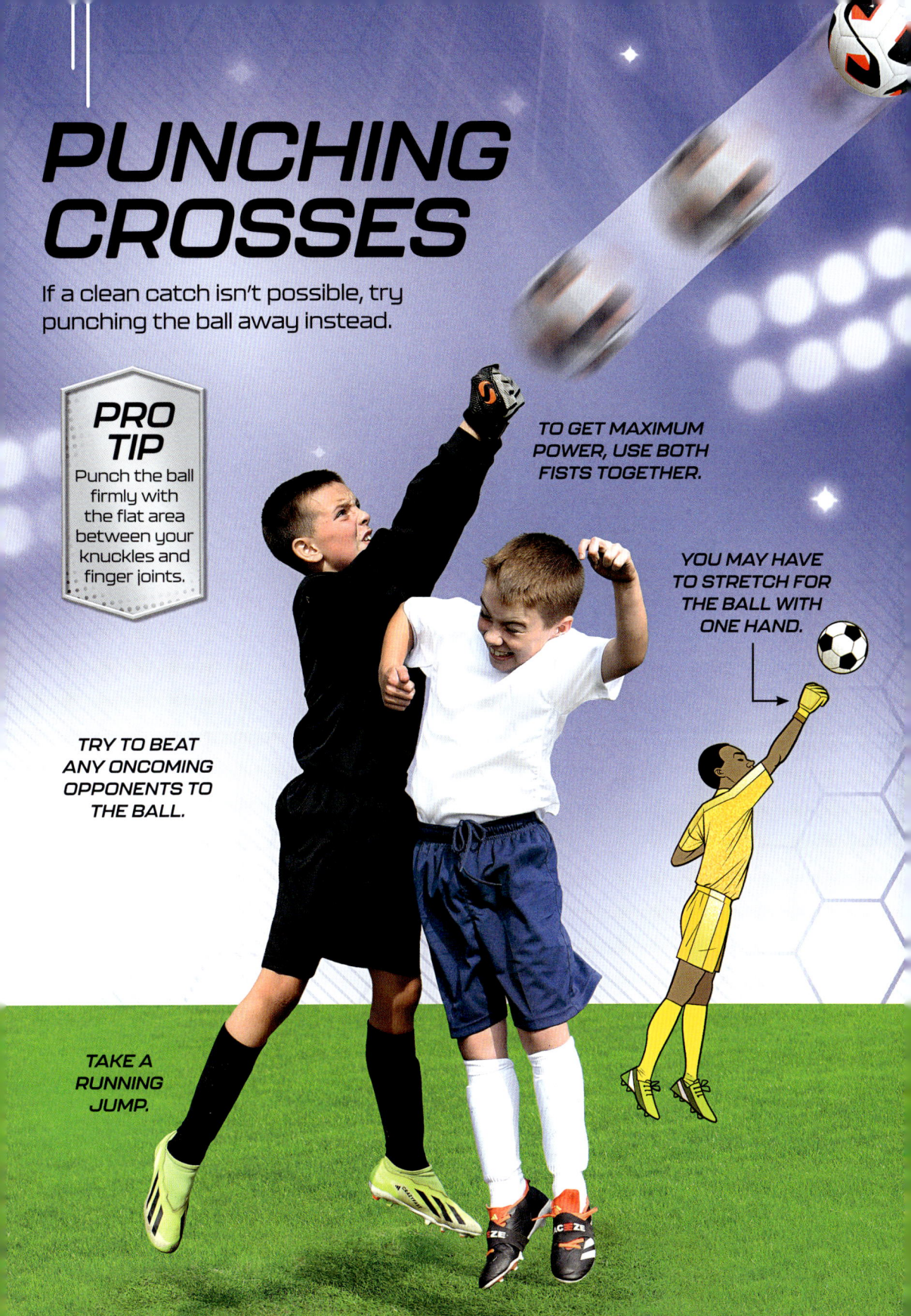

If a clean catch isn't possible, try punching the ball away instead.

PRO TIP
Punch the ball firmly with the flat area between your knuckles and finger joints.

TO GET MAXIMUM POWER, USE BOTH FISTS TOGETHER.

YOU MAY HAVE TO STRETCH FOR THE BALL WITH ONE HAND.

TRY TO BEAT ANY ONCOMING OPPONENTS TO THE BALL.

TAKE A RUNNING JUMP.

GOALKEEPING

TIPPING THE BALL

Some shots are too high to catch, but even just getting your fingertips onto the ball can be enough to prevent a goal.

SKILL LEVEL 7 OUT OF 10

KEEP YOUR WRIST AND FINGERS STIFF TO STOP THE BALL

TRY TO TIP THE BALL OVER THE BAR OR AROUND THE POST.

LAUNCH YOURSELF IN THE DIRECTION OF THE BALL.

QUICKLINKS
Watch videos of some amazing fingertip saves, and learn some extra tips.
usborne.com/Quicklinks

HAND POSITION

Keep your palm open and your fingers spread wide.

TIPPING A LOB

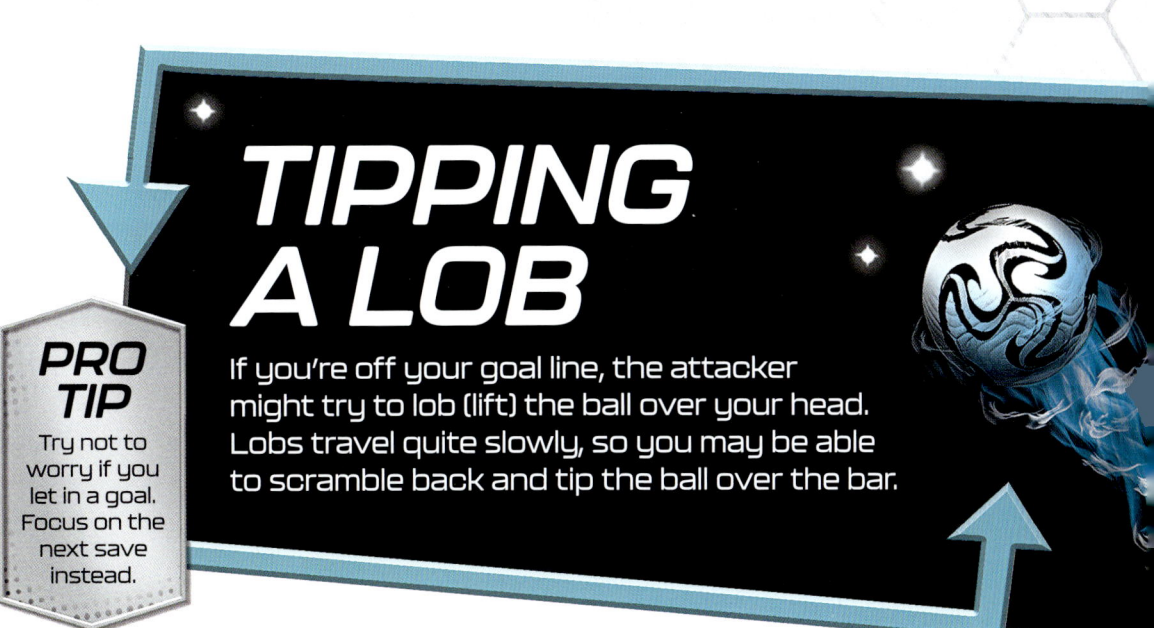

PRO TIP
Try not to worry if you let in a goal. Focus on the next save instead.

If you're off your goal line, the attacker might try to lob (lift) the ball over your head. Lobs travel quite slowly, so you may be able to scramble back and tip the ball over the bar.

Try this drill with a partner, to practise getting back in position.

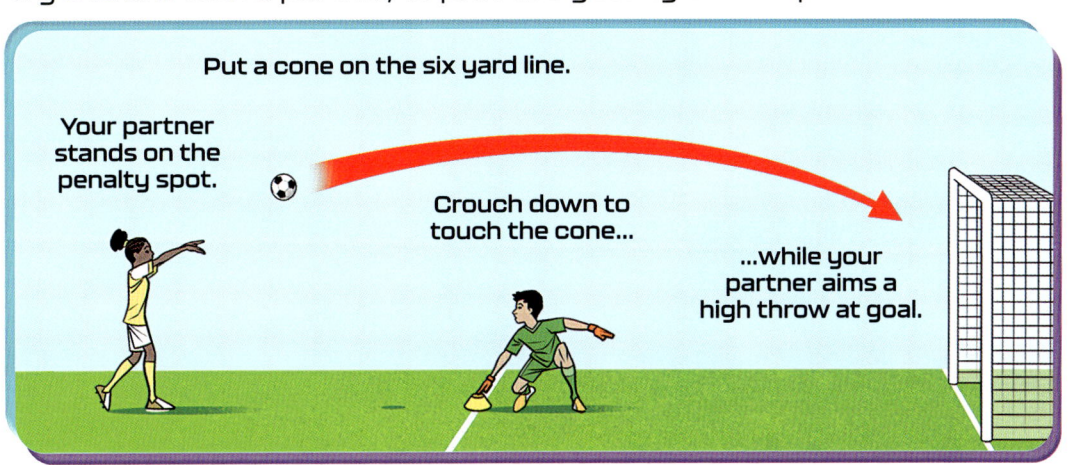

Put a cone on the six yard line.

Your partner stands on the penalty spot.

Crouch down to touch the cone...

...while your partner aims a high throw at goal.

Step back quickly...

...leap and reach up to tip the ball over the bar.

Keep your eyes on the ball at all times.

PLAYING TOGETHER

BEING A TEAM

Football is a team sport. To do well, you need to work together and support each other, both on and off the pitch.

EVERY PLAYER IS IMPORTANT. YOU WIN TOGETHER AND YOU LOSE TOGETHER.

LISTEN TO YOUR MANAGER OR COACH.

THEY'LL HELP YOU TO IMPROVE AS A TEAM.

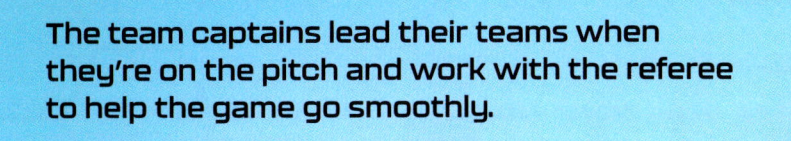

The team captains lead their teams when they're on the pitch and work with the referee to help the game go smoothly.

PRO TIP
The captain should be a positive role model for the rest of the team.

CAPTAINS SHAKE HANDS AT THE BEGINNING OF A MATCH.

ARMBANDS SHOW WHICH PLAYERS ARE THE CAPTAINS.

Celebrating a win is easier than handling a loss, but you'll have to learn to do both!

BE THERE FOR YOUR TEAMMATES WHEN THEY NEED YOU.

IN A GAME
Parents and carers can play a key role too, being positive and supporting the whole team.

95

PLAYING TOGETHER

THE RULES

The rules for football are known as the laws of the game. By following the rules, players all over the world can enjoy the same game.

QUICKLINKS
You can look up all the laws of the game in the FA Handbook.
usborne.com/Quicklinks

THE REF

The laws are enforced on the pitch by the referee. Referees can stop play by blowing their whistle, and have the power to show yellow or red cards.

A YELLOW CARD IS A WARNING.

If a player gets two yellow cards in the same game, it converts to a red card.

A RED CARD IS A SENDING-OFF.

The player must leave the pitch for the rest of the game, and can't be replaced.

THE REF POINTS TO THE PENALTY SPOT TO SIGNAL A PENALTY.

VAR

In some televised games, a Video Assistant Referee (VAR) might use video technology to help make decisions. If the referee isn't sure, VAR can offer a second opinion.

FREE KICKS

If a player does something that breaks the rules, the other side gets a free kick. There are two types of free kick, direct and indirect.

DIRECT

You can score directly from a direct free kick. If it's awarded in the penalty area, it's a penalty.

Reasons for awarding a direct free kick include:
- handball
- kicks, trips or pushes
- holding or barging an opponent
- biting or spitting at someone.

INDIRECT

You're not allowed to score directly from an indirect free kick. The ball has to touch another player first.

Reasons for awarding an indirect free kick include:
- obstructing an opponent
- preventing the goalkeeper from releasing the ball
- a player being offside.

OFFSIDE

Offside is when a player in the opponent's half is beyond the last defender when the ball is played, then goes on to touch the ball or get involved with play in some way. The assistant referee signals offside by raising their flag.

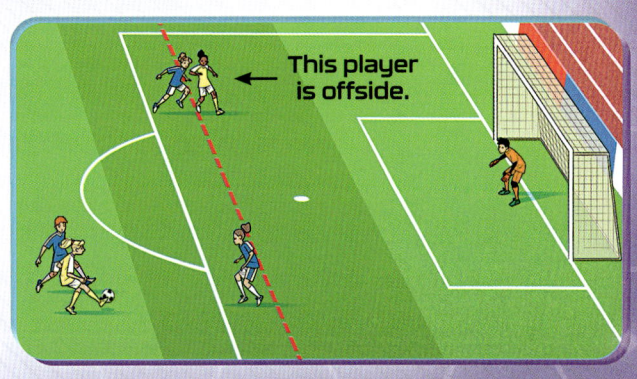

← This player is offside.

97

PLAYING TOGETHER

RESPECT

Everyone has the right to play, watch and enjoy football. As well as following the rules, it's important to show each other respect. No one should feel picked on or left out.

WARNING
Players who don't show respect will be asked to apologise. For serious offences, they could be sent off and suspended by their club.

IN A GAME
If an opponent is down with an injury, you can kick the ball out of play. This creates time to check if the player is OK.

AFTER A TACKLE, PLAYERS OFTEN HELP EACH OTHER UP TO SHOW NO HARD FEELINGS.

PRO TIP

Treat others on the pitch how you would like to be treated yourself.

PLAYERS SHAKE HANDS AFTER A GAME TO SHOW THEIR RESPECT FOR EACH OTHER.

CODE OF CONDUCT

QUICKLINKS
Read more about codes of conduct and the importance of respect.
usborne.com/Quicklinks

Players at all levels are encouraged to sign a code of conduct, agreeing to behave in a certain way. Here's an example:

When playing football, I will:

- Always play to the best of my ability
- Play fairly – I won't cheat, dive, complain or waste time
- Respect my teammates, the other team, the referee and my coach
- Play by the rules, as directed by the referee
- Shake hands with the other team and referee before or at the end of the game
- Listen and respond to what my coach tells me
- Understand that a coach has to do what is best for the team and not one individual player
- Talk to someone I trust or the club welfare officer if I'm unhappy about anything at my club

There's also a recommended code of conduct for parents, carers and supporters:

- Remember that children play for FUN
- Applaud effort and good play as well as success
- Always respect the match officials' decisions
- Remain outside the field of play and within the Designated Spectators' Area (where provided)
- Let the coach do their job and don't confuse the players by interfering
- Encourage the players to respect the opposition, referee and match officials
- Support positively. When players make a mistake, offer them encouragement not critcism
- Never engage in, or tolerate, offensive, insulting, or abusive language or behaviour

99

PLAYING TOGETHER

SHOW RACISM THE RED CARD

This book was written in collaboration with the anti-racism educational charity, Show Racism the Red Card. Red Card uses the high-profile status of football and football players to help tackle racism in society.

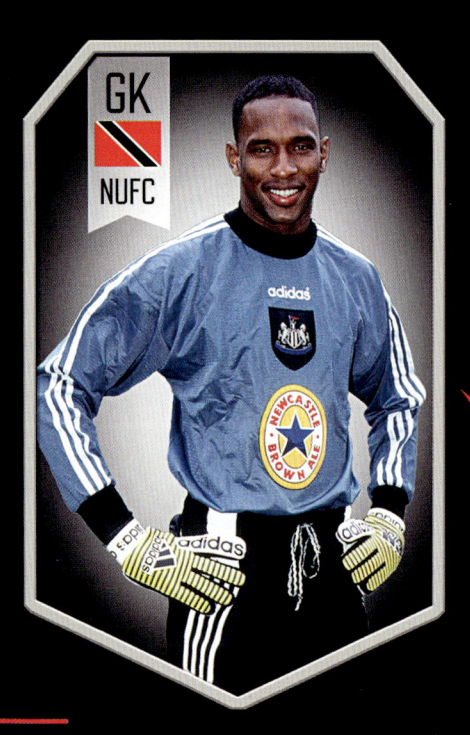

The charity was founded in the 1990s, inspired by footballer Shaka Hislop's own experience.

When Shaka was filling his car with fuel one evening, a group of local football supporters started shouting racial abuse at him.

As they got closer, they recognized who it was and their tone changed instantly. They didn't want to insult their team's star goalkeeper, they wanted his autograph!

"THAT'S WHEN I REALIZED I COULD HARNESS MY INFLUENCE AS A PROFESSIONAL FOOTBALLER TO MAKE A DIFFERENCE." SHAKA HISLOP

Shaka turned his negative experience into a positive one. He started visiting schools with his teammates to challenge racism through education.

Now Show Racism the Red Card delivers sessions to over 50,000 people a year, from children in schools to adults in their workplace to events in football stadiums.

BREAKING DOWN BARRIERS

There are many more opportunities for women and girls to play football today, but it's not always easy.

The expert adviser on this book, Naomi Bedeau, faced many challenges on her way to becoming a professional footballer. Here's just one example...

In the park one day, two boys took it in turns to pick players for their teams. Naomi was the only girl there and the last to be picked. When the game began, no one passed to her.

Eventually she intercepted the ball and let her football skills do the talking. Only then did the boys' attitudes to her change and she was finally included.

CB / NFFC

Naomi signed for Nottingham Forest FC in 2024.

"MY BROTHER GOT PICKED BEFORE ME, AND I'M MUCH BETTER AT FOOTBALL THAN HIM!"
— NAOMI BEDEAU

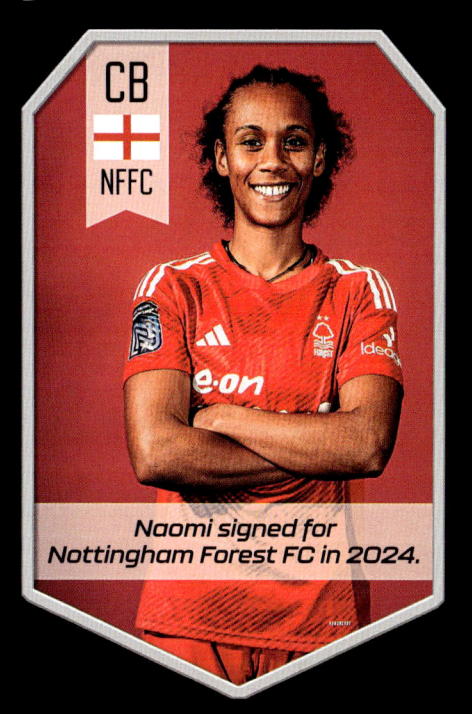

The young footballers in this book are from Oadby Owls Football Club in Leicestershire, UK.

The club is for girls and boys of all abilities, from the age of three. Its aim is to give everyone the opportunity to enjoy football in a safe and friendly environment.

"I AM IMMENSELY PROUD OF THE CHILDREN WHO HAVE PARTICIPATED IN THIS AMAZING INITIATIVE. INCLUSIVITY AND A SENSE OF BELONGING ARE EXTREMELY IMPORTANT IN THIS EVER-CHANGING WORLD. EVERYONE SHOULD FEEL VALUED, APPRECIATED, AND RESPECTED."
— HAF KATIB, CHAIRPERSON OF OADBY OWLS FC

GLOSSARY

Here are some of the key football words, and what they mean.

Clearance – when the ball is kicked or headed away from goal

Coach – a person who runs training sessions

Corner kick – a set play for the attacking team that's taken next to the corner flag

Cross – a sideways pass into the opposition's box from near the touchline

Dribble – run with the ball at your feet

Drill – a training routine

Feint – a trick where you pretend to dribble one way, then go the other. Or pretend to shoot and then don't.

Foul – something that's against the rules, e.g. a dangerous tackle

Free kick – a set play given when the other team commits a foul

Goal kick – a set play for the defending team when the ball comes off an attacker and goes wide of goal

Goal line – the line from one corner flag to the other, marking the end of the pitch

Instep – the top of your foot

Intercept – win possession by blocking an opponent's pass

Jockey – block your opponent's route to goal without tackling them

Keepy uppies or kick-ups – keeping the ball in the air without using your hands

Manager - the person who picks the players and the formation. Sometimes called the head coach.

Offside - a foul conceded when you play the ball forwards in the opposition half, but one of your teammates in the attack is closer to the goal than the last defender

One-on-one - when you're through on goal with just the keeper to beat

One-two - a quick pass to a teammate that lets you run past your opponent and collect the return pass

Penalty - a free kick for the attacking team that's taken from the penalty spot. All players except the taker and the keeper must stand outside the area.

Possession - when one team has control of the ball

Rebound - a loose ball that's bounced off the keeper back into the penalty area

Referee - the person on the pitch who makes sure both teams play by the rules

Set play - a pass or shot where the ball is put back into play after a stoppage, e.g. a free kick or throw-in.

Shielding - stopping the opponent from getting to the ball by putting your body in the way

Tackle - a challenge on the opponent when they have the ball

Throw-in - a set play taken from the touchline where you throw the ball to a teammate

Touchline - the line from one goal line to the other, marking the side of the pitch

Volley - a shot or pass when the ball is in the air

Wall - a line of defenders between the ball and the goal when a free kick is taken

103

CREDITS

HUGE THANKS TO...

Our football models – Amelia, Barney, Dawud, Delbir, Eleri, Ellie, Ganga, Gary, Harith, Harrison, Indi, Josh, Junior, Kaynat, Kerryn, Lexi, Munyaradzi, Nivaan, Rian, Shiv, Tanaya, Teale, Umar and William; Haf, Dean and Adhvait from Oadby Owls FC; Emma Haywood; Blaby & District Spartans FC; Leicestershire & Rutland County FA for the use of Holmes Park.

Cover design by Marc Maynard
Additional contributors: Gong Studios, Gill Harvey, Jonathan Sheikh-Miller, Richard Dungworth, Clive Gifford and Rob Lloyd Jones
Additional photo credits: Newcastle United FC (p100 top), Fulham Primary School (p100 bottom), Nottingham Forest FC (p101 top), Chris Bunce Studio (p101 bottom)

First published in 2025 by Usborne Publishing Limited, 83-85 Saffron Hill, London EC1N 8RT, United Kingdom. usborne.com. Copyright © 2025 Usborne Publishing Limited. The name Usborne and the Balloon logo are registered trade marks of Usborne Publishing Limited. All rights reserved. No part of this publication may be reproduced or used in any manner for the purpose of training artificial intelligence technologies or systems (including for text or data mining), stored in retrieval systems or transmitted in any form or by any means without prior permission of the publisher. UKE.